Praise for Sherry Argov's Work

"The Best of Culture."

D0950323

–*Esquire*

"America's top relationship guide."

—*The Book Tribe*

* * *

One of "The 10 Most Iconic Relationship Books of the Past Ten Years."

—*Yahoo!*

* * *

"We're talking about having so much self-respect, Aretha Franklin would high-five you."

—*Los Angeles Times*

* * *

"The pejorative meaning of the word 'bitch' has been reclaimed . . . it means a strong, feisty woman who has moxie, and knows when to use it. A bitch is like a Tarantino movie—sap free."

—*Pursuit Magazine*

* * *

"[Argov is] talking about a strong woman. Someone who knows what she's doing in life. Someone who will share the load, but who will stand her ground."

—Joy Behar, Co-host of *The View*

* * *

"Sherry Argov shows women how to transform a casual relationship into a committed one."

—*The Today Show*

* * *

"The whole Mary Ann vs. Ginger thing notwithstanding, men don't really go for 'nice.' They go for 'interesting.'"

—*Chicago Sun-Times*

Praise for Sherry Argov's Work

"A must-read at Sunday brunch."

—*New York Daily News*

* * *

"A hot new book!"

—*Fox News Channel*

* * *

"Sherry Argov's national bestseller, *Why Men Love Bitches*, flew off the shelves. . . . Men thrive with women who can set boundaries and who push back when they try to cross the line."

—*Cosmopolitan*

* * *

"An anti-whining manifesto that encourages women who feel like doormats to develop a sense of independence."

—*Playboy*

* * *

"If you've been too nice, run out and get this book now!"

—Ellen Fein and Sherrie Schneider,
authors of the *New York Times* Bestseller *The Rules*

* * *

"Her sassy book is filled with scenarios and advice aimed at making women subtly stronger and self-empowered. The book, which has already been featured on *The View* and *The O'Reilly Factor*, should make waves with its controversial view of relationships."

—*Publishers Weekly*

WHY MEN
LOVE
Bitches®

Sherry Argov

Avon, Massachusetts

Copyright © 2009, 2004, 2002, 2000 by Sherry Argov. All rights reserved.
This book, or parts thereof, may not be reproduced in any form
without permission from the publisher; exceptions are made
for brief excerpts used in published reviews.

Why Men Love Bitches is a registered trademark of Sherry Argov.

Published by
Adams Media, a division of F+W Media, Inc.
57 Littlefield Street, Avon, MA 02322 U.S.A.
www.adamsmedia.com
ISBN 13: 978-1-58062-756-6
ISBN 10: 1-58062-756-0

Printed in the United States.

10 9 8 7 6 5

Library of Congress Cataloging-in-Publication Data
Argov, Sherry.
Why men love bitches / Sherry Argov.
p.   cm.
ISBN 1-58062-756-0
1. Mate selection. 2. Single women—Life skills guides.
3. Self-esteem in women. 4. Dating (Social customs)
5. Man-woman relationships. I. Title.
HQ801 .A724 2002
646.7'7--dc21
2002009981

This publication is designed to provide accurate and authoritative information
with regard to the subject matter covered. It is sold with the understanding that
the publisher is not engaged in rendering legal, accounting, or other professional
advice. If legal advice or other expert assistance is required, the services of a com-
petent professional person should be sought.
      —From a *Declaration of Principles* jointly adopted by a Committee of the
American Bar Association and a Committee of Publishers and Associations

Many of the designations used by manufacturers and sellers to distinguish their
products are claimed as trademarks. Where those designations appear in this book
and Adams Media was aware of a trademark claim, the designations have been
printed in initial capital letters.

This book is available at quantity discounts for bulk purchases.
For information, call 1-800-289-0963.

Dedication
For Mom, with love.

CONTENTS

Acknowledgments

First and foremost, I thank and acknowledge my beautiful mother, Judy. Aside from being the best mother and my favorite person in this world, she taught me everything I know about how to be a strong woman, and how to see humor in everything. Making Mom proud is the only accomplishment that really matters.

I also want to thank the super teams at both Adams Media and F+W Media. I thank David Nussbaum, CEO and President of F+W Media. David Nussbaum is the kind of CEO someone is fortunate enough to work with once or twice in an entire career. I thank him for his special brand of leadership. I thank Chris Duffy, Royalties Manager at Adams Media, for being a consummate professional. I appreciate all the times he's gone the extra mile. I extend my gratitude to Sara Domville, President of the Book Division at F+W Media, and Karen Cooper, the newly appointed Publisher of Adams Media. How cool it is to see two great women at the helm. I offer special thanks to Stephanie McKenna, Foreign Rights Manager at Adams Media, who is the reason this book is selling in so many languages. I recognize Amy Collins, former Director of Sales at Adams Media, as the talented mind who originally led the book-launch efforts; she is my dear friend.

I want to thank Edward Colbert of Looney & Grossman, who is my brilliant lawyer, advisor, and counselor. I thank him for being in my corner, and for being someone I can *always* count on.

I want to thank my accountants, Kathryn Schmidt of Schmidt & Co., and Ali Adawiya of SongCare. They are both geniuses. I thank Dan Dydzak, lawyer and friend, for his friendship and pep talks at the local diner.

I want to thank Jeff Hyman, my photographer. His kindness will always be remembered. I thank Christine Serrao, of the Artist Relations department at MAC cosmetics, for her gracious help with my TV makeup.

I thank my special guy, who is my rock. (Fortunately for me, he doesn't read these kinds of books or take me too seriously.) Nevertheless, I thank him for his great suggestions on what I "really need to tell those bitches" after spending a day with "the guys."

I thank my favorite relatives who watch over me like angels: Tova, Samuel, Arnon, and Yossi Chait.

I thank my readers—my sisters—who tell all their girlfriends about my books, and who have taken the time to write me letters. I thank the good men out there who were kind enough to share how men think. The best part about writing a book such as this is meeting interesting people with a great sense of humor. I thank them for the privilege.

Introduction

Why Men Love Bitches is a relationship guide for women who are "too nice." The word *bitch* in the title does not take itself too seriously—I'm using the word in a tongue-in-cheek way representative of the humorous tone of this book.

The title and the content address what many women think, but don't say. *Every* woman has felt embarrassed by appearing too needy with a man. *Every* woman has had a man pursue her, only to lose interest the minute she gave in. *Every* woman knows what it feels like to be taken for granted. These problems are common to most women, married and single alike.

So why do men love bitches? An important distinction should be made between the pejorative way the word is usually used, and the way it is used here. Certainly, I'm not recommending that a woman have an abrasive disposition. The bitch I'm talking about is not the "bitch on wheels" or the mean-spirited character that Joan Collins played on *Dynasty*. Nor is it the classic "office bitch" who is hated by everyone at work.

The woman I'm describing is kind yet strong. She has a strength that is ever so subtle. She doesn't give up her life, and she won't chase a man. She won't let a man think he has a 100 percent "hold" on her. And she'll stand up for herself when he steps over the line.

She knows what she wants but *won't* compromise herself to get it. But she's feminine, like a "Steel Magnolia"—flowery on the outside and steel on the inside. She uses this very femininity to her own advantage. It isn't that she takes undue advantage of men, because she plays fair. She has one thing the nice girl doesn't: a *presence of mind* because she isn't swept away by a romantic fantasy. This presence of mind enables her to wield her power when it is necessary.

In addition, she has the ability to remain cool under pressure. Whereas a woman who is "too nice" gives and gives until she is depleted, the woman with presence of mind knows when to pull back.

Among the hundreds of interviews I conducted with men for the book, over 90 percent laughed and agreed with the title within the first thirty seconds. Some men chuckled as though their best-kept secret had just been revealed. "Men need a mental challenge," they said. Time and time again, this was the recurrent theme.

The men I interviewed all phrased it slightly differently, but the message didn't change. "Men like it when a woman has a bit of an *edge* to her," they said. Two things became clear across the board: First, they would regularly use the phrase *mental challenge* to describe a woman who didn't appear needy. And second, the word *bitch* was synonymous with their concept of *mental challenge*. And this characteristic, above all, they found attractive.

When I used the phrase *mental challenge* with men, it was immediately clear to them the quality I meant. On the other hand, when I interviewed hundreds of women, rarely did they understand the same phrase. They often related the phrase to intelligence, rather than to neediness. It wasn't just that my hunch was confirmed by these interviews; they also strengthened my sense of purpose. I thought that anything this *obvious* to men should not be kept a secret from women.

This book addresses the very issues that men *won't*. He

won't say, "Look, don't be a doormat," "Don't always say yes," "Don't revolve your whole world around me." This book is necessary because *these are things a man will not spell out for his partner*.

In the chapters that follow, you'll find one message coming through loud and clear: Success in love isn't about looks; it's about attitude. The media would have us believe differently. A teenage girl picks up a magazine and reads: "Get that boy's attention" with an item of clothing, or a certain look. "This nail color or lipstick will wow him," the magazine assures her. And what does the girl learn? How to obsess over someone else's approval.

Then there is the issue of how the media treats aging. The teenage woman evolves into a twenty-something woman with confidence, and the media bombards her with negative images of aging. The message here is: Two wrinkles and a stretch mark, and she's "marked down" like last season's merchandise that's sold at half price. And what does she learn? How to obsess over someone else's *disapproval*.

So what's the message of this book? It's that a bit of irreverence is necessary to have any self-esteem at all. *Not irreverence for people, but rather, for what other people think*. The bitch is an empowered woman who derives tremendous strength from the ability to be an independent thinker, particularly in a world that still teaches women how to be self-abnegating. This woman doesn't live someone else's standards, only her own.

This is the woman who plays by her *own* rules, who has a feeling of confidence, freedom, and empowerment. And it's this feeling that I hope women will glean from reading this book.

The woman who has a positive experience with men possesses the ever-so-subtle qualities I discuss in this book: a sense of humor and an aura that conveys, "I'm driving the train here. I'll tell you where we get on and where we get off." This woman has that presence of mind to do what is in her best interest and an attitude that says she doesn't need to be there. She is there *by choice*.

The bitchy women who are so loved by men give off a devil-may-care quality and, yes, have that "edge." This is that same edge, coincidentally, that men say they find so magnetic. The difference is this woman isn't looking for it outside herself; it is a special quality she carries within.

Note: Throughout this book, some names have been changed at the request of those interviewed.

1

FROM DOORMAT
TO
Dreamgirl

Act Like a Prize and You'll Turn
Him into a Believer

" Sex appeal is 50% what
you've got, and 50% what
people *think* you've got. "
—SOPHIA LOREN

Meet the Nice Girl

Everyone has known a "nice girl." She is the woman who will overcompensate, giving everything to a man she barely knows, without him having to invest much in the relationship. She's the woman who gives blindly because she wants so much for her attentions to be reciprocated. She's the woman who goes along with what she thinks her man will like or want because she wants to keep the relationship at all costs. Every woman, at some point, has been there.

Certainly, the average fashion magazine gives women ridiculous relationship advice that makes it easy to understand why women are so eager to overcompensate: "Play hard to get, then cook him a four-course meal . . . bake him Valentine's cookies with exotic sprinkles shipped from Malaysia (just like Martha Stewart). Don't forget the little doilies and the organic strawberries that you drove two hours to get. Then serve it all to him on the second date, wearing a black lace nightie." And what is this a recipe for? *Disaster.*

ATTRACTION PRINCIPLE #1
Anything a person chases in life runs away.

Especially when it comes to dealing with a man. With one caveat: If you chase him in a black nightie, first he'll have sex with you . . . and then he'll run.

Why does a man run from a situation like this one? He runs because the woman's behavior doesn't suggest that she places a high value on herself. The relationship is new, and the bond between them is relatively shallow. Yet she's already dealt him her best card.

The fact that she is willing to overcompensate to a virtual stranger immediately suggests one of two things. He'll either assume she is desperate, or he'll assume she is willing to sleep with all men right away. Or *both.* What gets lost is his appreciation for her extra effort. Once a man begins to lose respect for a woman because she is willing to subtly devalue herself, he will also lose the desire to get closer to her. Nightie or no nightie.

A dreamgirl, on the other hand, won't kill herself to impress anyone. This is why the woman he really falls in love with doesn't serve a four-course meal. And you won't see her breaking out the fancy china, either. She'll start out cooking him a one-course meal. (Popcorn.) No fancy doilies. A Tupperware bowl does the trick. She simply asks her guest, "Hey, do you want the bag or the bowl?" Six months later, the same woman throws together a meal and puts down a hot plate in front of him. And what does he say to himself? "Man! I'm special!"

It doesn't matter if it is pasta with Ragu topped by a meatball you picked up at the corner deli. He'll say, "This is the best pasta I have ever had in my life!"

Now he feels like a king. And the only difference is the amount of time and effort he had to invest, first. He didn't get it all right up front and he appreciated it more.

ATTRACTION PRINCIPLE #2
The women who have the men climbing the walls for them aren't always exceptional. Often, they are the ones who don't appear to care that much.

This isn't about how to play a game or how to manipulate someone. This is about whether you are genuinely needy, or whether you can genuinely show him that you'll be an equal partner in the relationship. It's about whether you are capable of *holding your own* in a relationship.

What would happen if you let him know from day one that you are willing to bend over backward? He'd think you're desperate, and he'd want to see just how far you'd be willing to bend. It is human nature. He'd immediately start to test the waters. The more malleable you'd become, the more he'd expect you to bend. He'll instantly perceive you as a Duracell battery, as in, "Just how far will she go? How much can I get out of her?"

Nice girls need to know what a bitch understands. Overcompensating or being too eager to please will lessen a man's respect; it will give the kiss of death to his attraction, and it will put a time limit on the relationship.

Most men don't perceive a woman who jumps through hoops as someone who offers a mental challenge. Intelligent women make the mistake of assuming that if they hold a higher degree, they can hold their own in a political debate, and they have a good understanding of mid-caps, they offer a man mental stimulation during dinner. But the mental challenge has little to do with conversation. (Granted, if she thinks that Al Green and Alan Greenspan are the same person, then Houston? We have a problem.)

In general, the mental challenge has to do with whether you expect to be respected. It has to do with how you relate to him. It has to do with whether he knows that you aren't afraid to be without him.

The nice girl makes the mistake of being available all the time. "I don't want to play games," she says. So, she lets him see how afraid she is to be without him and he soon comes to feel as though he has a 100 percent hold on her. This is often the point when women begin to complain: "He doesn't make enough time for me. He isn't as romantic as he used to be."

A bitch is more selective about her availability. She's available sometimes; other times she's not. But she's nice. Nice enough, that is, to consider his preferences for when he'd like to see her so that she can *sometimes* accommodate them. Translation? No 100 percent hold.

What about the woman who will drop everything and drive to see a man? The man also knows he has a 100 percent hold on her. After a couple of dates, he goes out with the boys, comes in at midnight, calls her, and off she goes to see him. When a woman drives to see a man in the middle of the night, the only thing missing is a neon sign on the roof of her car that says WE DELIVER.

ATTRACTION PRINCIPLE #3
A woman is perceived as offering a mental challenge to the degree that a man doesn't feel he has a 100 percent hold on her.

Your time with him is telling. The nice girl sits in a chair after a week of knowing the guy, bored out of her mind as he does something that interests him. He may be watching sports on TV, cleaning his fishing gear, strumming his guitar, or working on his car. She is miserable but doesn't say a peep. Instead, she tries to make the best of it and twiddles her thumbs politely, just so she can be in his company.

The bitch, on the other hand, makes plenty of peeps. In fact, she is bitching the whole way through. This is not a bad thing, because then he knows he can't walk all over her. But remember, a mental challenge has little to do with being verbally combative. It has to do with your actions and how much of yourself you are willing to *give up*. For example, he says he likes blondes. You have dark skin, dark eyes, and black hair. The next time he sees you, you've bleached your hair and dyed your eyebrows to match. Translation? He'll sense he has a 100 percent hold on you.

"A man's love comes from his stomach," they say. That's true, but no one said to slave for six hours to feed him. Whether he eats out or you order take-out, the stomach is full, and there is plenty of love to go around. Rule of thumb: If it is warm, he'll eat it. The rest is wasted effort.

Women are conditioned to give themselves away. I have yet to see a men's magazine with an article on how to cook a woman a four-course meal. The closest they ever come to a recipe is in the bodybuilder section, when they tell guys to mix up a few egg whites with some wheat germ.

I raise the issue of cooking because it's one of many ways that women overcompensate. This doesn't mean you should forgo cooking altogether. Perhaps it's your anniversary, and you've been together a whole year. Perhaps it is his birthday, and you want to do something special for him.

On a special occasion, and after he has earned it, cooking him a meal is a nice "treat." But it isn't a treat if you give it to him right off the bat. Since this is a book for women, I would be remiss if I didn't include some recipes for those first weeks in a relationship. And, unlike Martha Stewart's recipes, the following are easy to remember. You don't even need recipe cards.

Appetizer
Popcorn à la Carte

I recommend popcorn for its convenience and quick preparation time. First, place the bag in the microwave. When all the kernels have popped, remove the popcorn from the microwave carefully, because it will be very hot. Be sure to wear a cooking mitt, an apron, and a spatula to assist in the removal of the popcorn from the microwave. This will not only impress your guest, it will also make it look like you really know what you're doing.

If you find that the popcorn is burned, notice *where* it is burned. If it's black at the top, dump out the black part and salvage the rest by pouring it into a bowl. Serve the yellow part to your guest, and then adjust the time when you make a new bag for yourself.

Serves: one and a half. (Good enough.)

Main Course

Gourmet Delicate Dippings

Bring a pot of water to a boil, and plop in two wieners. Cook them for five minutes so the wieners are tough or slightly *al dente*. Pour your guest a refreshing beverage (Kool-Aid). Then send him onto your balcony so he can enjoy the lovely view—as ambience is everything. When he isn't looking, slice and dice the little wieners and stick a toothpick into each piece. Like Martha, you can truly express your creativity with a wide assortment of different colored toothpicks. Now serve the little wieners with two "delicate dipping" sauces, served side by side: ketchup and mustard. And never refer to them as weiner slices, always refer to them as "Gourmet Delicate Dippings."

Now for dessert: a jelly roll (Hostess) served with coffee (instant). And an after-dinner mint always makes a classy finishing touch. I recommend peppermint, spearmint, or Trident.

You'll know dinner was a smashing success when he insists on taking you out to eat next time. Never again will you hear him utter the words, "Hey, what's for dinner?"

If, after some time, he ever slips and asks you to cook, simply offer to make your specialty: popcorn, wieners, and a jelly roll, with coffee and Kool-Aid to help wash it down. Then start getting ready because you'll have reservations within the hour.

The bitch is not the woman who will sit at home and work overtime to refine her "man-catching" skills. All she feels she has to do in the beginning is focus on being good company. This is more than enough until he earns the "catbird seat" at the top of the yacht.

In the beginning, pay close attention and take note of the following: If he's unwilling to lift a finger during the courtship, he is showing you right up front that he has nothing to offer you in the future. This behavior has nothing to do with your worth. It has everything to do with what he has to offer. And it also has to do with how you present yourself. Are you working overtime? If he has a lot to offer but you don't allow him to come your way, he'll have no other option but to back off. When a nice girl overcompensates, her behavior says, "What I have to offer isn't enough, and who I am isn't enough." The bitch, on the other hand, gives a very different message. "Who I am is enough. Take it or leave it." And now, a comparison:

"I AM NOT ENOUGH." VS.	"I'M ENOUGH. TAKE IT OR LEAVE IT."
She calls him often and says, "Please return my call."	She gets back to him when she's free.
She is on call like a rookie flight attendant.	She sees him when it is convenient for her.
She makes it obvious a relationship is her goal before she knows much about him.	She goes out to have fun and doesn't make promises to a virtual stranger.
When he does call her, she is mad he didn't call sooner.	When he calls her, he is curious where *she* is, and why she's not there.

(continued)

"I Am Not Enough." vs.	"I'm Enough. Take It or Leave It."
She often drives.	He'll pick her up or happily go out of his way.
She asks, "Where's our relationship going?"	He has no clue where the relationship is going, and she leaves it like that.
She talks about having babies.	She can't remember his last name.
She asks him about the "ex."	He brings up the ex; she looks at her watch.

One = Doormat   **The Other = Dreamgirl**

The foundation is laid from day one. From the very beginning, he consciously (yes, consciously) tries to figure out what the parameters are *and how much he can get away with*.

Phone etiquette is also telling. Do you wait to hear from him before you make plans? Do you get bent out of shape if he doesn't call, check in, or show up as expected?

If so, you are not giving him a lesson in punctuality. What you are doing is showing him he has a 100 percent hold on you, which isn't a good message to give someone you've just met.

It's a fact that most men deliberately don't call, just to see *how you'll respond*. When a woman is upset, she is easy to read. And a man can easily gauge how much a woman wants or needs the relationship by simply pulling back a little bit. So forget all those other theories from magazines about why men don't call.

ATTRACTION PRINCIPLE #4
Sometimes a man deliberately won't call, just to see how you'll respond.

It is human nature for a man to test the waters to see how much he can get away with. You see it in the behavior of children and even in the behavior of pets. It's par for the course.

Pulling back is also something men do to gain reassurance. No man is going to say, "Honey, I need reassurance about where I stand with you." Instead he'll pull back to see how you'll react. When you react emotionally, it gives him a feeling of control. And if you react emotionally frequently, over time he will come to see you as less of a mental challenge. If he can't predict how you'll always react, you remain a challenge.

It also gives him something he absolutely needs: the freedom to breathe. If you don't hear from him for a little longer than usual, show him that you have absolutely no "attitude" about it. This behavior will make him a little unsure about whether you miss him (i.e., "need him") when he isn't around. It gives him a reason to come your way because he won't perceive you as needy.

Try not to say things such as "Why haven't you called me?" or "Why haven't I heard from you in a week?" If you act as though you haven't even noticed (because time flies when you're having fun), he will come your way. Why? Because he doesn't feel as though he has a 100 percent hold on you.

A top teen magazine recently gave women the following bad advice. They said to slip notes in unexpected places like his backpack or locker, or to "write a poem and slip it under his windshield wiper." As if this wasn't enough to give his attraction the kiss of death . . . Wait, it gets better. In addition, they advised catching him off guard by "having a pizza delivered." Okay. Put it all together and what do you get? A magic recipe for convincing him you are a *stalker*.

ATTRACTION PRINCIPLE #5
If you start out dependent, it turns him off. But if it is something he can't have, it becomes more of a challenge for him to get it.

Again, it isn't about learning how to play a game. It's about understanding human nature and behaving accordingly. A man will always want what he can't have. When a man meets a woman and she seems nonchalant, it becomes a challenge for him to win her affections.

Or, if he tries to get a woman to react in an insecure way but she holds herself with a level of dignity and pride, suddenly the dynamic changes. The same guy who was gun-shy of relationships becomes a believer. Now he begins to fantasize about getting the so-called bitch to cook him a meal, fold his socks, or chase him around. But if you *start out* dependent on him, he simply doesn't value it the same.

Another mistake that a woman can make is to put herself down. When you're on a date, you should never talk about the plastic surgery you want to have or the weight you want to lose. Don't talk him out of a compliment. This is the time to be sure of who you are.

So, what's the right attitude? "This is me, in all of my splendor . . . and it doesn't get any better than this." Don't spend a fortune on a therapist. Just say it to yourself until you believe it. Eventually you *will* believe it, and so will he.

Humility? Don't worry. It's a treatable affliction, a mental glitch. If you catch yourself being modest or humble or any of that nonsense, correct the problem immediately. Go directly back to believing you are "a catch." Period. End of story. Case closed. If someone else doesn't like your confidence, that's their problem. *Why?* *You always come before they do, that's why.*

Case in point: Ever hear a man say that all the guys wanted his ex-girlfriend? He'll build her up so much that when you finally see a picture, you are dumbfounded. What you really want to say is, "Honey, she looks like she had the starring role in *Lassie Comes Home.*" Don't bother because he'll rush to her defense: "She looked better in real life." No sale . . . try again. "She looked better back then? (Pause.) It was a really bad picture, no, really." (Still, no sale.)

What women need to understand is that when a man considers a woman to be a prize, looks have very little to do with it. In the above example, it was a simple mind trick that goes like this: She acted like a prize, and then a funny thing happened. He completely *forgot who he was looking at.*

ATTRACTION PRINCIPLE #6
**It is your attitude about yourself
that a man will adopt.**

The same works in reverse. A beautiful woman can make herself look ugly in the eyes of a man if she is very insecure.

He pursued you; therefore, he finds you attractive. An understated demeanor and a confident attitude will convince him you're gorgeous.

Never assume you are not attractive enough, and therefore you have to overcompensate or chase a man. Taste is subjective. One man's "ugly" is another man's "beautiful." The first date is about looks. When he falls in love, it's about your attitude. It's about whether you can hold your own. Which is all about how you hold *yourself.*

ATTRACTION PRINCIPLE #7
Act like a prize and you'll turn him into a believer.

A woman also demeans herself when she compares herself to another woman. So, don't let on when you feel threatened by another attractive woman who walks into the room. If you want to make a woman who is a 6 on a scale of 10 look like a 12, what do you need to do? Simple. Act threatened by her. If you pretend not to notice her, he'll see your confidence in yourself and then he'll become intrigued with *you.* Then another curious thing will happen. Suddenly she won't look so good. She only has as much power as you give her.

A girlfriend of mine named Samantha went on a first date with a man who took her to a local boxing match. In between rounds, as always, there was a sexy, barely dressed stripper who came out holding the round number. Her date looked at the woman and then, in an effort to be a gentleman, turned to look at Samantha. She acted as though she was oblivious as to why he had turned to look at her.

When the woman came out again in the following round in a see-through lace nightie, my friend leaned down under the seat and nonchalantly asked her date if she could drink some of the water in his water bottle. He said, "Sure." At no time did she behave as if she was threatened. Instead, she remained very composed as though the other woman didn't even exist. By the end of the third round, he no longer noticed the woman in the boxing ring.

The end result was that he was completely enamored with Samantha. And while driving home, he kept saying how incredibly beautiful he thought she was. The proof was in the pudding. He continued to pursue her, not the stripper who overcompensated, to get the kind of attention *that is often very short-lived*.

While my friend's behavior was exemplary, his wasn't all that romantic. It should not go unnoticed that a man is willing to take you somewhere unromantic on the first date. If a man takes you to a boxing match, a strip joint, or a place he might typically hang out with a bunch of guys, he's telling you by the choices he is making that he doesn't plan to have you around that long. If this is where he takes you on a first date, *don't* go out with him a second time.

If you are in an uncomfortable situation, don't feel compelled to compete with another woman. In addition, you don't need to expose a lot of skin or feel as if you have to work harder to earn a man's sexual attention. I know a woman who takes off layers of clothes based on how the other women in the room are dressed. The issue again is overcompensation. No need.

Wearing your sexuality on your sleeve isn't advantageous in luring a man. The issue is not about whether you are successful in turning him on; this is no big achievement. He can get aroused from riding a motorcycle or from sleeping. The issue is not whether you turn him on; it's whether he *stays* turned on *after* he has been satisfied. This is the key.

Quality men are attracted by less, not more. If he sees a pretty secretary wearing her hair in a bun, right there in broad daylight he's going to start wondering what she looks like with her hair down. If he sees a woman dressed in a way that shows there is something moving behind a sweater that he can't see, his desire to see is greater than if she's showing it right off the bat. When you show your shape, but don't expose every inch, the "unwrapping of the gift" becomes much more stimulating. If he has to unbutton an item of clothing to get to what he wants to see, it turns him on *more*. Not less.

You often hear a man say of a provocatively dressed woman, "I wouldn't kick her out of bed for eating crackers." This is true until he's had "his way" with her and then crackers or no crackers, he moves on. The difficult part isn't getting a man's interest. The trick is knowing how to *sustain* it.

Much of holding your own in a relationship begins with *how you hold yourself.* Overcompensating is overcompensating, and it includes everything from calling a man too much to cooking a four-course meal to dressing too provocatively. Remember the saying: The candle that burns twice as bright burns half as long.

If, at a later date, you dress provocatively, that's another story. Then he knows you are doing it just for him, so it becomes a treat. This is why you often hear men say they want a lady in the living room and a whore in the bedroom.

It's what you don't show that keeps him intrigued.

Don't let the advertisements on TV be your guide. The woman who sustains a man's interest is not the one who feels confident because of a particular miniskirt, a belly ring, or a black dress with a plunging neckline. A bitch doesn't rely on these things to feel good about herself. She relies on *who she is as a woman*.

"He should accept me as I am!" says the woman who is too nice. Accept you? Oh no, sister. Slap yourself. He should want you madly. Acceptance has nothing to do with it. He *accepts* a doormat. But he *desires* his dreamgirl. If you want acceptance, go to a self-help group. We're talking about what he craves. It started when he was a kid. When he received a toy for Christmas that he didn't even ask for, he played with it for a whole five minutes. The toy he cherished was the one he bought with two months' allowance that sat on the top shelf in the toy store. He couldn't reach it but went in to look at it all the time. He got up every morning at the crack of dawn to toss papers on a paper route to get that toy. It's the one toy he will always remember because he had to earn it.

In Her Mind	In His Mind
"I am going the extra mile."	"She is trying too hard. She's desperate."
"I don't want to play games."	"She talks too much."
"I am nurturing."	"She is mothering."
"I am giving 100 percent so I can make it work."	"She is *really nice*, but there just isn't any chemistry."

But with the bitch? There's no lack of sexual chemistry.

She Has That "Je Ne Sais Quoi"

Je ne sais quoi is a French expression that translates to "I don't know what." It implies "that something special" that there aren't words for. It is that elusive charming quality you just cannot put your finger on. What does this quality boil down to? A woman who is comfortable in her own skin and cannot be made to feel bad about herself.

It isn't about looks; gorgeous women get dumped every day. It isn't about intelligence. Women of all types, from brilliant women to women with the IQ equivalent of plant life, pull it off every day. It's about mystery and learning how to create intrigue.

When you lose your *edge*, the relationship loses its *fire*. Think of him as the match. You are the striking board on the back of the match cover. When the rough edge or sand wears off and starts to become dull, it is much harder to get that spark.

For example, the man may say, "Maybe I need a little time to think things over." The woman who is too nice responds, "Please don't leave me." Not the bitch. She offers to help him pack. Why (choose *A, B,* or *C*)?

A. She is helpful.
B. He can't pack.
C. She loves herself.

Hint: The correct answer is *C*. Because she loves herself, the bitch doesn't want anyone who doesn't want her. She doesn't grab his ankles and beg for mercy. She keeps that edge. And, in doing so, she prevents him from wanting to go.

Her aura says she doesn't want him desperately enough, need him desperately enough, or let him get under her skin enough. She is driving that train. *Effortlessly*. And it is that very ease that translates into charm.

Je ne sais quoi is a sexy devil-may-care attitude. Not only isn't the bitch needy of him, she often isn't focused on him.

Ever notice that when you are on the phone ignoring the man you are with, suddenly he'll kiss your neck and try to get your attention? Ignore him and he is intrigued. Make him the center of attention all the time and he runs.

ATTRACTION PRINCIPLE #8
The biggest variable between a bitch and a woman who is too nice is *fear*. The bitch shows that she's not afraid to be without him.

Margaret Atwood said, "Fear has a smell, as love does." It is said that excitement and fear come from the same part of the brain. When a man is slightly afraid of losing a woman, his excitement is piqued.

His psyche is like a plant. It needs water but also air to breathe. To give a man too much reassurance too soon is the same as overwatering a plant. It kills it.

One of the things women have to get out of their mindset is the notion of what a bitch is. A bitch is *nice*. She's sweet as a Georgia peach. She smiles and she is feminine. She just doesn't make decisions based on the fear of losing a man.

The difference between the bitch and the nice girl is not

so much in their personalities or in their demeanor. It has nothing to do with how abrasive a woman is. A bitch is a bitch with her actions, because she isn't willing to give herself up.

ATTRACTION PRINCIPLE #9
If the choice is between her dignity and having a relationship, the bitch will prioritize her dignity above all else.

The bitch remains the person she is throughout her relationship with a man. She doesn't lose her friends. She doesn't give up her career or her hobbies. She doesn't give up all of her time or bend over backward. And, unlike the nice girl, she is not *too tolerant* of disrespect.

She also keeps her edge and has enormous self-respect; she holds the conviction that her self-worth governs her decisions. Because she is not afraid, ironically he becomes *afraid to lose her.* Because she is not needy, he starts to need her. Because she isn't dependent on him, he begins to depend on her. It's like a reverse magnet. The person who is least dependent on the outcome of the relationship will automatically draw the other person in.

Meet the "New and Improved" Bitch

Let us conclude this chapter by redefining the word *bitch.* Think of it as a "term of endearment." A bitch is not a woman who speaks in a harsh tone of voice. It is not a woman who is abrasive or rude. She is polite but clear. She communicates directly with a man, in much the same way men communicate with one another. In this way, it's easier for a man to deal with her than with a woman who waffles or appears too emotional, because the emotionally sensitive type of woman confuses him. The bitch knows what she likes and has an easier time expressing it directly. As a result, she usually gets what she wants. Here are the ten characteristics that define her.

1. *She maintains her independence.*
    It doesn't matter if she is the CEO of a company or a waitress at Denny's. She earns an honest living. She has honor, and she isn't standing there with her hand out.

2. *She doesn't pursue him.*
    The moon and the sun and the stars don't revolve around him. She doesn't make her dates with him when her horoscope advises that his big Mercury is about to retrograde in her little Venus. She doesn't chase him or keep tabs on him. He is not the center of the world.

3. *She is mysterious.*
    There is a difference between honesty and disclosure. She is honest but does not reveal everything. She isn't verbally putting her cards on the table. Familiarity breeds contempt and predictability breeds boredom.

4. *She leaves him wanting.*

   She doesn't see him every night or leave long messages on his machine. She isn't on a first-name basis with his secretary in one week. Men equate longing with love. Longing is good.

5. *She doesn't let him see her sweat.*

   She keeps communication from getting messy and avoids communicating when upset. When she clears her head, she is succinct and speaks in a "bottom line" way.

6. *She remains in control of her time.*

   She takes it slowly, *especially* when he wants to hurry. She moves to her rhythm, not his, preventing him from taking control of her.

7. *She maintains a sense of humor.*

   A sense of humor lets him know she is detached. However, she doesn't treat disrespect as a laughing matter.

8. *She places a high value on herself.*

   When he gives her a compliment, she says thank you. She doesn't talk him out of it. She doesn't ask what the ex looked like and doesn't compete with other women.

9. *She is passionate about something other than him.*

   When he feels he isn't the "be all and end all" of her existence, it makes her more desirable. Staying busy ensures she isn't resentful if he is unavailable. He doesn't have a monopoly on the rent space in her head. He doesn't get Park Place, and he doesn't get Boardwalk. He gets one of those little purple properties next to Go.

10. *She treats her body like a finely tuned machine.*
   She maintains her appearance and health. A person's self-respect is reflected in how he or she maintains physical appearance. If he tells her he doesn't like red lipstick, she wears it anyway, if it makes her feel good.

2

WHY MEN *Prefer* BITCHES

Cracking the Code:
What Every Nice Girl Needs to Know

> " Happiness? A good cigar,
> a good meal, a good cigar,
> and a good woman—or a
> *bad woman.* It depends on
> how much happiness you
> can handle. "
>
> —GEORGE BURNS

The Thrill of the Chase

Women need to understand that men love the "thrill of the chase" and are highly competitive. They like racing cars, engaging in athletics, and hunting. They like to fix things, to figure things out, to pursue.

The cat-and-mouse game that women find maddening is actually very exciting to men. This is a very basic difference between the sexes. For a woman, the objective is often a committed relationship, also known as the destination. For a man, the road trip *on the way* to the destination is often the most fun.

The bitch understands that when a man wants something he'll go after it, and going after it makes him want it even more. If he doesn't succeed right away, he starts to crave it. It captures his interest and excites his imagination. A woman who is too nice throws cold water on this process. A man is more likely to get bored when he hasn't really invested much of himself.

No one respects a freebie or a handout in any facet of life. When a woman sleeps with a man right away, it doesn't pull him in. The men I interviewed often admitted that if the sex was too easy to get, it was not that great.

It's like blackjack. If he wins big right up front, he's done for the night. But with the slow win, things develop differently. He wins a few hands and then loses a couple. At this point, wild horses couldn't pull him away, because he feels so close to winning again. He can almost taste it. His inborn, competitive male nature kicks in and makes *him stay there and fight*. And if he's losing, he'll fight even harder.

ATTRACTION PRINCIPLE #10
When a woman doesn't give in easily and doesn't appear docile or submissive, it becomes more stimulating to obtain her.

Another example is when he goes on a hunting trip with "the boys." They go out for a whole week. He sleeps in a grungy sleeping bag and gets chewed up by mosquitoes. He eats food that prison inmates wouldn't touch. For what? The hunt. Then if he actually kills a moose, he comes home prouder than a peacock and wants to hang the moose head on the wall in the den. (Look out—the hunter is now a decorator.)

Let's notice something, because it is significant. If you were to drop a dead moose on his doorstep, he'd want nothing to do with it. It could be the very *same moose* he had hunted, and yet it could have a totally different effect on him. This is how the pursuit affects his interest in a woman. When a woman chases a man, it has the same effect as if she were to deliver a dead moose to his front door.

The objective while dating is not to be mean. It's to give him the thrill of the chase by taking it slowly and letting him *be a man*. It's easy to understand his nature because it is our human nature, too.

ATTRACTION PRINCIPLE #11
Being right on the verge of getting something generates a desire that has to be satisfied.

Men often admit, "You always want what you can't have." The bitch never lets him feel that he has her under his thumb. Since he never quite has her, he never stops pursuing her.

So when he thinks he's making progress and he has you right where he wants you, sometimes it's appropriate to gently remind him that you aren't under his thumb. Here are just a few comparisons between the nice girl and the bitch.

SCENARIO #1: HE CALLS YOU AND EXPECTS YOU TO BE AT HOME.

If the nice girl leaves, she calls first to tell him where she'll be and what time she'll be back.	The bitch lets him think about where she is every now and then.
Often she'll assure him that her cell phone's on, should he want to get ahold of her.	She lets him wonder if she's outside his reach by not always reporting her whereabouts.

SCENARIO #2: HE SAYS HE'LL CALL AT AROUND A CERTAIN TIME AFTER HE GETS IN. THE CALL IS FOUR HOURS LATE.

The nice girl yells at him and says she was worried. "You should have called!"	The bitch isn't so easily upset, so she isn't so easy to read. She may or may not pick up the phone, which makes him miss her.

SCENARIO #3: HE SEEMS A LITTLE WITHDRAWN, PENSIVE,
AND NOT PARTICULARLY TALKATIVE.

The nice girl continually pries and asks, "What are you thinking about?" She worries that he is pulling away.	The bitch is in her own thoughts. She doesn't panic, which makes him come her way.

SCENARIO #4: HE IS VERY LATE FOR A DATE AND
KEEPS HER WAITING.

The nice girl waits, calls him on his cell phone four times, and tells him he should "value her more."	The bitch waits a half-hour and then makes other plans.

The difference in these situations isn't as much how you treat him as how you treat yourself. The bitch's behavior lets him know without any words that she will not pull the plug on her life to accommodate him.

Are You *Too* Nice?
A Pop Quiz

---

1. Do you feel guilty when you say no, or do you say no and then second-guess yourself?

   Yes   No

2. Do you often try to tell your partner that you want to be treated with respect?

   Yes   No

3. Do you find yourself bartering or negotiating for what you want or need?

    Yes   No

4. Do you often pass up sleep or the need for personal time to meet his needs?

    Yes   No

5. Do you regularly see him on short notice or when it is convenient for him?

    Yes   No

6. Do you find that you repeat what you've asked for as though he didn't hear it the first time?

    Yes   No

7. After a fight, are you always the first one to contact him or apologize?

    Yes   No

8. Do you find you are much more doting and affectionate than he is?

    Yes   No

9. Do you often feel depleted after he has been with you?

    Yes   No

10. Do you constantly want more attention or reassurance?

    Yes   No

If you've answered yes to five or more of these ten questions, you are giving far more than you are receiving. Let's explore why giving yourself up is never in your best interests.

Women understand the concept of balance between work

and play. They balance time with family and time with friends. They balance a job with getting an education. But when it comes to a man, the nice girl abandons all sense of balance and immediately makes the man the whole pie. But with a bitch, he is just a piece of it. She keeps the other pieces intact.

It all starts out subtly. "What are you doing right now?" he asks when he calls her from his cell phone. "Well, I was going to catch a movie with a girlfriend," she answers. The operative word is *was* (past tense). Then he asks, "Want to hook up?" She pauses for two seconds. "Okay."

A man will try to get you to be very accessible because it's natural that he'll want to make things more convenient for himself. And he'll do so by saying the following to pressure you to accommodate him:

"I don't like to plan things."
"I like to be spontaneous."
"I like to fly by the seat of my pants."

Another key factor that distinguishes the nice girl from the bitch is how much of herself she'll give up. Once you're in a relationship and he's shown a pattern of being interested over time, then it's okay to be a little more spontaneous. In the beginning, however, don't make yourself so accessible. If you do, the relationship will always be on his terms.

The nice girl will often cancel plans with a girlfriend if she gets a last-minute date. The bitch will hold her own simply by keeping her previously set plans. I know one bitchy woman whose partner absolutely adores her. If she's painting her toenails when he calls, she'll still say, "Thank you so much, but I'm a little busy right now."

ATTRACTION PRINCIPLE #12
**A man knows which woman
will give in to last-minute requests.**

Sometimes a man will get tickets to something at the last minute. Or he'll plan a romantic surprise. He is spontaneous, but clearly you're his first priority—so this is harmless. You're in good shape if he's calling you all the time and wants to see a lot of you.

What you want to guard against is going on last-minute dates or getting those last-minute calls to do something because he didn't have anything better planned. Sometimes when a woman has feelings for a man, she can't distinguish between the two.

THE SPONTANEOUS GUY WHO IS TREATING YOU LIKE A BACKUP	VS. THE SPONTANEOUS GUY WHO ADORES YOU
You don't hear from him for two weeks at a time and then all of a sudden you get a phone call.	He makes dates ahead of time, and he also wants to see you spontaneously in between.
He prioritizes social engagements with his drinking buddies.	His buddies complain that he fell off the face of the earth. They hassle him but he doesn't seem to care.
He makes travel arrangements with friends and never asks you to accompany him.	He's constantly asking you to take time off from work so you can get away together.

(continued)

THE SPONTANEOUS GUY VS. WHO IS TREATING YOU LIKE A BACKUP	THE SPONTANEOUS GUY WHO ADORES YOU
He's irritable when he's around you and frequently complains of not having more time to himself.	He's happy to be in your company. His friends and family all think he looks happier than he's ever looked.
He calls you to cancel plans for that evening. Later that night, you call right back and it goes directly to voice mail. Then he calls the following day with a good excuse.	If he has to cancel, he feels badly about it. He calls you when he gets in from wherever he is because he has nothing to hide and he *wants* you to know he's being totally "on the level."
He won't ever take you out or spend much money. He may ask you for a loan. Before you know it, you're supporting the guy through college.	He'll do anything just to see you smile.
You make it known that you're available on a weekend night. And even though he works during the week, he doesn't make himself available to see you.	He almost always sees you whenever you have time, unless he has a professional commitment or there's an important extenuating circumstance.

A common example is the typical "booty call." First, the guy waits to hear back from someone *else* before confirming whether he can see you. He'll call at 5:00 and say he hasn't showered yet and he's on the way. At 7:00 he calls again and pulls the plug: "My friend Troy stopped by." Then he says he'll make it an early night with Troy and tells you he wants to get together afterward. He gets in late, and that's when he offers to see you, providing you drive to his place.

No matter how much you want to see him, don't go. At this point, you want to *seriously* consider not ever seeing him again. If you do go, you won't be more appealing to him; you'll be turning the dimmer switch down on his attraction for you.

A friend of mine named Crystal was in this exact situation and handled it perfectly. A man named Brett called her on a Saturday night; it was well after midnight and raining, and he asked her in a seductive tone of voice to drive to his place. A classic booty call. Crystal hadn't heard from Brett in two weeks, since he'd indicated he wanted to "see other people." He also lived 35 miles away from her at the time.

Crystal said, "Okay, sweetie. I'm on my way. Give me five minutes to put on a garter belt under my raincoat. I'll be there in forty minutes." She also asked Brett to wait downstairs for her in the rain with an umbrella, so she wouldn't get drenched walking to the front of his apartment complex. He waited and waited and waited. Three hours later, it occurred to him like a stunning revelation: No booty cometh.

In the morning Crystal awoke to several messages from Brett. In one of them, he mentioned that he had come down with a severe case of the flu from standing in the rain. (Not her fault. He should have gotten his flu shot.)

Again, the bitch is very nice. She is as sweet as a Georgia peach. But inside every sweet peach is a strong pit. And this means she won't explain the obvious when a man is disrespectful. There is no way to hold your own in a relationship and simultaneously accept rude behavior. A quality man doesn't want a woman he can trot all over. There is nothing wrong with having a little self-respect—and a few conditions.

Condition #1.
He books in advance.
The message? Your time and attention are valuable.

If you treat yourself as a valuable commodity, he will naturally put more stock in you. For example, he calls and says, "When can I see you?" Don't say, "I'm wide open around the clock. Pick a time. *Anytime!*" He suggests Friday. "Okay!" He suggests Tuesday. "Okay!" He suggests three weeks from next Sunday. "Okay!"

Instead, politely tell him you have two nights that are good for you. Then let him choose one. He'll probably choose both.

Here's a similar circumstance. A doctor I know started a private practice. He didn't want his receptionist to say, "Sure, we have tons of openings. Drop in any time." Instead, he instructed her to say, "We can get you in at 2:15 or at 4:15. Which would work for you?" Most people would tend to value an appointment more with a doctor who appears to be fairly busy *but is willing to accommodate them* than with one who is always open like an all-night convenience store.

Condition #2.
Don't see him when you are "running on empty."
The message? He does not come before basic necessities (i.e., rest).

He says he'd like to see you at 9:00 P.M., and you don't want to be out too late? Tell him, "I'd prefer to get together earlier." If he can't because he is working late, make no issue of it. Simply suggest getting together another night.

Condition #3.
If you aren't having fun or he isn't good company, end the date immediately, and give a superficial explanation as to why.
The message? You have a standard of how you expect to be treated.

For example, you are on a first date. He gets drunk and behaves badly. For starters, never get into a car with someone who is drinking. Always keep a credit card in your back pocket or a $20 bill in your bra. Tell him you are going home early. Excuse yourself, go to the little girl's room, and call a cab.

Another friend named Kelly snagged a guy whom a lot of women wanted by setting the tone from the very beginning. She did so simply by being reticent. The man was extremely successful, very attractive, and charismatic. He first saw Kelly when he was eating his lunch at a cafeteria where she often eats. He had that confident vibe and was used to women hitting on him.

Kelly was the exception to the rule. He was trying to get her attention while she remained absolutely riveted by her BLT sandwich. She knew that he was watching her, but she pretended not to notice. He came back Tuesday. And Wednesday. And Thursday. When he finally asked her out, she paused before she answered, "I don't know you, so I can't look at you in a romantic way. We could start as friends and see where it leads."

Here's a guy who was used to women clamoring to be with him, but with Kelly, he was presented with a challenge to pursue a woman who let him know she won't be so easily won over. In this way, she *held her own.*

ATTRACTION PRINCIPLE #13
**Whether you have terms and conditions
indicates whether you have options.
Almost immediately, you present yourself
as a doormat or a dreamgirl.**

"Terms and conditions" are a novel idea for the woman who is too nice. (And you shouldn't leave home without them.) Don't get me wrong: Unconditional love is a beautiful thing. Just be sure to give it *after* your conditions have been met.

The Mama/Ho Complex

In the field of psychoanalysis, there's a male hang-up called the Madonna/Whore Syndrome. Let's forget all the fancy psychobabble and refer to the informal Mama/Ho version to better understand our male counterparts.

The Mama/Ho theory holds that a man will either see you as his "mama" or his "ho." The word *ho* is a derivative of the word *whore*. It is not a garden tool. A ho is any woman he is having sex with, any woman he wants to have sex with, or any woman he has had sex with.

The antonym for ho is mama. A man will feel affectionate toward a woman who is really sweet and nice, much like the affection he has for his mother. Because she doesn't present a challenge and she's always there, he begins to take her for granted. This is when you hear men say, "She's really nice, but there just wasn't any chemistry." Therefore:

SAFE + BORING + MAMA = *NO SPARK*

&

UNPREDICTABLE + NOT MONOTONOUS + HO = *FIREWORKS*

Even though a man is turned on by the independent woman he can't have, he'll still try to get you to be like his mama. He'll want you to cook, clean, and do his laundry.

One woman I know nipped the issue of laundry in the very beginning. Early in her marriage, she threw a red sweatshirt in with all of her husband's white cotton underwear. Then she turned the water on hot to seal the deal. The only underwear he had left was the pair he was wearing. No self-respecting, heterosexual male would ever be caught dead wearing *pink* underwear. On seeing the ruined garments, her husband threatened her with the very words she wanted to hear, "You will never, ever, ever do my laundry again!"

What a nice girl should know is that even if you make every effort to be an exemplary housekeeper, he'll still want a ho behind closed doors. The two are related. Why? Constant mothering will eventually turn a man off. Yes, they say that every man is looking for his mother. This is a nice theory, but it doesn't mean you should run out and do his laundry or treat him as though you are his keeper. There are four things that make a man feel suffocated or mothered, that often turn him off, and that make him distance himself from you like a rebellious teenager. These are the major Mommy no-no's:

Do not appear to check up on him or ask him to check in with you.

Do not expect him (without asking first) to spend all his free time with you.

Do not ask him to account for the time that he isn't with you.

Do not be overly doting, leaving him no room to come your way.

Never give the appearance that you are closing in on him. For example, suppose he gets off the phone with his long-lost Auntie Mae. If you immediately start questioning him or you jump down his throat and demand to know who was on the phone, it has the same effect as throwing on an apron and assuming the role of mama. Like a teenager, he'll rebel.

There are many things women inadvertently say that sound very motherly: "Get some rest," "Don't stay out late," "Call me when you get in," or "Eat something before you go out." You will make him feel *emasculated*. It's no different than telling a two-year-old, "After naptime we'll have a little cookie."

Asking a man to explain himself or check in with you is mothering. Maybe he ran a half-hour late coming home. Perhaps he was having a friend help him fix his lawnmower, or maybe he was having a beer under the hood of his friend's car. The very second he thinks he has to explain himself to you, he'll feel as though he is losing his freedom. Then he'll make up a story to conceal something that didn't need to be concealed, just to protect his "territory" or his "turf." And he'll feel cornered.

ATTRACTION PRINCIPLE #14
**If you smother him, he'll go into defense mode
and look for an escape route
to protect his freedom.**

Don't make him feel as though he has to ask permission for the day-to-day things he wants to do. It's smothering to him when you watch him too closely. Don't give him the feeling he's *under a microscope.* He'll feel controlled and will instantly want to get away.

When he's shaving and he's late for work, don't push your way into the bathroom to watch him. Don't look in his car's glove compartment as though there's something suspicious in there. Don't appear to eavesdrop on his phone conversations. Don't try to take over his kitchen or leave girlie things in his bathroom as though you're marking your turf. Don't ask him to spend all his time with you, and don't say, "I miss you" when he hasn't seen you in two hours. If you do these things, *you are subtly doing the chasing.*

Don't say things like, "Tuck in your shirt," "Go wash your hands," or "Go brush your hair." Don't ask him if he's hungry three times in a row, and don't wait on him hand and foot—unless he has a cold. (One little sniffle and you can treat it like a terminal illness.)

Don't plan all of your weekends together so he has to ask permission to go fishing. Let him catch a couple of fish. Otherwise, he'll start to break dates. Why? Because he's acting like a rebellious teenager who's been given a curfew by mama. He'll do it deliberately so you don't get used to *dictating* how his time is spent.

When you treat your time together as something he *has* to do, you've taken something that was a pleasure and made it a chore. If you are nice, but you give of yourself with strings attached, the demand for reciprocity will send him several steps backward. Whenever you make him feel as though he *has to* see you, it will feel like work. When it's *not* an obligation to see you, the very same thing will feel like pleasure.

ATTRACTION PRINCIPLE #15
Whenever a woman requires too many things from a man, he'll resent it. Let him give what he wants to give freely; then observe who he is.

Men like things that are difficult. They like to drive stick-shift automobiles. They like to jump out of airplanes, and they like to climb mountains. They like to do the impossible. Therefore, when he has to go out of his way to see you, he is actually happier. It will not feel like work to him.

This theory applies to anything—a phone call, time together, sex, or whether he checks in at the end of the day. If you always make him feel he has plenty of space to do his own thing, he'll always feel that lust. You'll be like a lover not like his mother. He'll perceive you as a privilege rather than an obligation, and he'll come your way.

The No Cage Rule

The minute a man feels vulnerable, he fears being devastated emotionally. When he meets a nice girl, she could potentially represent "forever." Heaven forbid she lets the word *relationship* trip off her tongue a couple of times? Call 911. He immediately thinks she wants to latch onto him and have babies. Heaven forbid you get excited to see a cute baby? Trauma. He has nightmares and sees it as a sign that he's in dire need of a backup form of birth control.

Sometimes you hear men say, "I want to leave my options open" or "I don't want to get tied down." Or they use catch phrases like *ball and chain* or *henpecked*. My favorite is a hyphenated term that begins with a female body part and is followed by the word *whipped*.

ATTRACTION PRINCIPLE #16
A bitch gives a man plenty of space so he doesn't fear being trapped in a cage. Then . . . he sets out to trap her in his.

Clearly, men are scared to death of losing control of their freedom. The thought of being stuck with one woman frightens them. If a woman immediately acts as if she *expects* a man to behave like a serious boyfriend without much effort on his part, he'll get scared and run off. With the nice girl, it only takes a few dates for him to feel trapped. And then "lockdown mode" begins.

WHAT SHE SAYS . . .	WHAT HE HEARS
"I'd love it if you'd let me know where you are at night. It's just common courtesy."	Limited supervised outings followed by check-in time with the warden.
"I get upset when you don't call me when we aren't together."	The *ringing* of the keys that are attached to his ball and chain.
"We should be together. Why do you need the boys if you have me?"	"Lights out and lockdown" in fifteen minutes!
"I'd like to get married and have kids within a year."	Nothing. (Inmate on the loose.)

Suddenly, *poof!* The magic is gone. He panics about being an inmate crammed into a cell. By contrast, the bitchier woman is a little more aloof, so it appears as if she has far less interest in taking away his freedom or locking him down. This is one of the major qualities that attract a man to a bitch.

Ask yourself the following . . .

- Ever have a pillow fight and notice that you and your partner are more turned on?
- Ever notice that when you play-wrestle with a man, he gets all fired up?
- Ever notice when a man steps over the line and you put him in his place, he gets turned on?
- Ever wonder why the men you *aren't* interested in won't stop chasing you?
- When you're dating someone and you don't pay attention to him, does he seem more intrigued and chase you even more?
- Have you ever played with your pet and noticed that your man seems jealous?

To fully understand these occurrences, we must focus our attention on where the true answer lies: The Animal Channel.

Men are hunters, and like any hunting animal, they are more intrigued by conquering prey when it resists the predator. Most men are turned on by a bitch because it's a thrill to take down a powerful woman.

Let's look at how this has practical applications. A grad student named Nancy was taking an evening class, and she had an interest in a male classmate. He kept sitting closer and closer until finally he asked her out. She said, "Okay, I'd love to. But while we are in this class, I just want you to know that I'd like to keep it professional." There was clearly an undeniable amount of chemistry between them, so her comment was hardly a deterrent. It became: Operation Get That Girl.

ATTRACTION PRINCIPLE #17

**If you tell him you are not interested
in jumping into a relationship with both feet,
he will set out to try to change your mind.**

The way to quell his fears is to say you aren't interested in anything "too serious." As long as you appear interested in him, he'll keep coming your way. In his mind, you'll always be able to be convinced otherwise because men are so conditioned to meeting women who want commitment. By not appearing to want commitment, you throw a monkey wrench in the lockdown program. He no longer knows what to expect.

Things You Can Say to Avoid the Cage

When you go on a first date, tell him you "don't want to be in a serious relationship, for the time being." (Of course, things may change.)

When you work together, say, "I don't know if it's a good idea for us to mix business with pleasure." (You need a little convincing.)

When it's a long-distance relationship, say, "I'm not sure long-distance relationships can work." (Tentative is good.)

This is how you get in the conductor's seat of the train, and this is when he wants to stay on board. When he's driving, there is no "thrill" and no "chase." But when you're driving, suddenly it's a fun ride because he can't anticipate what will happen next. (I submit to you, my fellow sisters, it's very selfish *not* to indulge him in so much fun.)

The opposite is also true. If, for example, you *don't* like him and wish he'd stop calling, try, "Babies? I love babies! I want at least a half a dozen of them, maybe more. My clock is ticking so I'd like to have them soon. *Real soon.* Perhaps six of them in the next four years . . ." Keep talking about those babies.

This is the perfect approach for that friendly guy you aren't interested in and you don't want to hurt. It's a perfect way to get rid of him. "Diapers? It's easy to get the hang of it. And, don't worry . . . you'll get used to the smell of the poop!

It won't last too long, just until they get potty trained . . . ." Just make sure you're on the ground floor when you tell him, so he doesn't get hurt when he jumps off the balcony. (Open windows and high altitudes should also be avoided.)

If you don't make him feel locked down, he'll come your way. Think of him as a frightened stray dog. Eventually, he'll drop his guard and come around. But if you charge at him or try to corner him, he'll bolt.

This also relates to why men prefer bitches. When he meets a woman who is unavailable or a little bitchy, he has a built-in excuse for why he isn't going to get too close. "She's a bitch, so I won't get too serious. I'll just have a little fun," he says to himself. Fun equals freedom. That is, until he gets attached and then it's checkmate. Men don't *choose* to be in love. It happens by accident. That's why they coined the phrase *to fall in love*. As in "Oops!" He *fell*. He had a plan . . . but it went terribly awry.

ATTRACTION PRINCIPLE #18
**Always give the appearance
that he has plenty of space.
It gets him to drop his guard.**

The more relaxed he is, the less guarded he'll be; and then it's only a matter of time before he reaches the point of no return. When he's in madly in love, you won't need to say things like "Where are you going?" or "What are you doing?" He'll tell you everything you ever wanted to know because he *wants* to, not because you had to ask. And, if and when he does go out with the boys, he won't be able to wait to get home to you.

The Power of Choice

Who can forget the scene in *Coming to America* in which Eddie Murphy, as the prince, stands before the altar prepared to wed his beautiful bride in a prearranged marriage? Before the ceremony, he takes the bride into a back room and asks her, "What do you like?" She responds, "Whatever you like." Then he asks her what she likes to eat. "Whatever you like." Her answers become more and more subservient. Then he tells her to bark like a dog and hop on one leg. When she does, he realizes he can't go through with the wedding.

A man wants a woman who has a mind of her own. An *opinion.* The way you assert yourself lets him know whether you have self-confidence. It lets him know you can hold up your end of the bargain. When he gives you a "little crap," you can give him a "little crap" right back. He respects a woman who can "trade blows" with him *and hold her own.*

You don't have to always agree with everything he believes. A man falls in love with a woman when he feels he has "met his match."

If you feel strongly about something, don't be afraid to say so. When he asks, "What movie do you want to see?" don't always tell him to choose. How about saying, "Hey, I sat through two of your 'shoot-'em-up-bang-bang' movies, so we're seeing a 'chick-flick' tonight." Men are attracted to a woman who can speak her mind. As one married man described, "Sometimes, get dressed to go out and tell *him* to stay home with the kids. Don't ask him. *Tell him.*"

Another said something even more poignant. "I don't think most men would mind if a woman was the one in control at home. Just as long as no one else knew about it."

So begin your dating relationship with a voice. Don't give the impression you are spineless. Remember the scene in *When Harry Met Sally* when Meg Ryan's character takes an hour to order her sandwich? Have an opinion. State a preference. Be polite, but don't be afraid to express yourself.

For example, suppose you're at the video store deciding between two movies to rent. Don't get the one that you've already seen. "I'll see it again if you haven't seen it." Slap yourself. "There are a lot of good movies. How about we get one neither one of us has seen?"

If he suggests Indian food and you absolutely hate it, say, "Hey, I heard there's a really good new restaurant right next door." Show him that you aren't afraid to make a suggestion or take the initiative. Assume that a man wants to be a gentleman. And if he wants to be a gentleman, he wants to *please you*.

The bitch requires an equivocal situation, whereas the nice girl does not. If the guy insists on picking the movie or restaurant all the time and has no regard for what she likes, the bitch will not have any contact with him. It isn't about Italian or Chinese. It isn't about one movie over another. It's about whether he shows her he is selfish. This is a character flaw the bitch won't tolerate.

This is a silly example, but I'll offer it because evidently it worked. A Swedish girlfriend of mine named Anna recently had dinner with a man, and he ordered two lobsters. The waiter brought the two live lobsters to the table and asked, "Will this be okay, sir?" My friend is not a vegetarian, but she grew up with a couple of pet frogs in Sweden and was alarmed to see the lobsters' little legs kicking. She said, "I just couldn't sit through the next five minutes knowing these two things would be boiled alive," and she insisted that he change the order.

Anna would have bet her life savings that this guy would never call her again, but he did. He called almost every day that week. He wanted to please her more than he wanted lobster. That's a gentleman. I'm not saying the lobster example is a trick you should try at home, but it's far better than the Eddie Murphy bride who said, "Whatever you like."

ATTRACTION PRINCIPLE #19
More than anything else, he watches to see if you'll be too emotionally dependent on him.

It isn't that a man wants a woman who is "bitching" all the time or complaining about everything that's wrong in her life. He wants a woman who isn't afraid to disagree or express an opinion.

When he asks on the first date, "What do you like to do?" don't shrug and say, "Um. You know. Stuff." You don't need to say you'll bungee jump, climb mountains, and then come home and have sex all night. But show him that you have an "appetite for life." *Your life.*

It's all in how you describe things. "Occasionally, *(yawn)*

I pick up a book." This not the same as "There is this *amazing* book I'm reading by Susan Faludi, and it's so intriguing. She's such an incredible writer."

To better understand why men are put off by needy women, keep this example in mind. Ever had a girlfriend who always comes around when she is upset over some guy? In between relationships, she is nowhere to be found. After not hearing from her for two months, she cries on your shoulder when the guy blows her off. Then you don't see her again until the next guy dumps her.

Eventually you won't want to be around her because you *won't feel as though she is contributing* to your friendship. That's how a guy feels when you are too dependent on him. It becomes a burden if you lean on him too much. He is only human, and he has his own problems. Show him that you'll be an equal partner, which means that you also have something to contribute.

ATTRACTION PRINCIPLE #20
He must feel that you choose to be with him, not that you need to be with him. Only then will he perceive you as an equal partner.

The mere fact that the bitch can throw a little weight around or put him in his place once in a while gives him the impression she doesn't need to be with him. She can stand on her own two feet. So, instead of feeling as if he's lost his freedom, he feels as though he's gained a strong woman. The relationship is a contributing force, rather than an obligation he's stuck with.

This is also why giving him space is so important. It makes you look proud rather than desperate. It enables you to remain a challenge indefinitely. Why? You *chose* to be with him. You didn't *need* to be. As a person, you feel you are complete with him or without him. This is the most important thing you can convey: independence rather than dependence. This is what gives him the perception you can *hold your own*.

3

THE
Candy
STORE

How to Make the Most of
Your Feminine and Sexual Powers

" Sex is like a small business.
Ya' gotta watch over it. "

—MAE WEST

One Jujube at a Time

If you look at the run-of-the-mill survey of what men find attractive in a woman, you'll get the basic, boring, predictable answers: "Studies have concluded that what men look for is . . . appearance, chemistry, and the way a woman carries herself." What a shocker!

Then you turn the page. "Buy a new lip gloss . . . pluck out all your eyebrows and draw them back in . . . stick three vials of collagen in your glossed-up lips . . ." And this will get him eating out of your hand, right? Not in *this* life. You'll be right back where you started but with no eyebrows.

Ever wonder why you see a gorgeous guy marry the girl-next-door? To your eye she looks plain, but to his eye she's a "natural beauty." It doesn't matter if her most glamorous moment was winning the Miss Pumpkin Patch contest on a farm at age six. When he goes to bed with her, he's happier than a fat rat in a cheese factory.

In general, there are two things a woman does to encourage a man to fall madly in love *after* he is attracted to her. First, she appeals to his imagination, sexually. Second, she waits a little while before consummating the relationship, sexually. This brings us to the "candy store" theory: *Don't give up the candy store at once. Give it one jujube at a time.*

ATTRACTION PRINCIPLE #21
**If a man has to wait before he sleeps
with a woman, he'll not only perceive her
as more beautiful, he'll also take time
to appreciate who she is.**

What men don't want women to know is that, almost immediately, they put women into one of two categories: "good time only" or "worthwhile." And the minute he slides you into that "good time only" category, you'll almost never come back out.

It's not that the bitch is slutty or more conservative—it's that she demands that he treat her as though she is "worthwhile." And, more often than not, it means revealing her sexuality a little at a time.

With her demeanor, the bitch is subtly "driving that train." Because he perceives her as slightly standoffish, he knows a lot of other men can't get to her. In fact, he's not even sure if *he* can have her. So he'll rarely get the luxury of being able to assume that she's a "good time only" companion.

The doormat is more likely to be perceived as a pushover sexually because she's more likely to sleep with a man for the wrong reasons—and *much* too soon. It has nothing to do with whether she appears conservative. Whether her style is long skirts and a ponytail and she attends napkin-folding class—or she wears sexy clothes and seems like a party girl—the outcome can be the same. In either scenario, if she has sex with a man because she feels she *needs to do so in order to win him*, he'll sense it and begin to lose respect for her.

A man named Brad described this distinction: "There are two types of sexy. The woman who is obviously *trying* to be sexy. Then there is the woman who *isn't trying* to be sexy—she just is. Most guys find the second one to be much sexier. It may not seem like that, because the woman who is *trying hard* will get you to do a double-take because she's more obvious about it. But the woman who isn't trying is sexier. And that's the girl you'll take seriously."

What is more interesting is that Brad is just out of college. And if a guy in his early twenties saw this with 20/20 vision, rest assured—so will most men you meet.

The following table shows how a man can quickly make these observations with relatively little information. Note that both types of women exude sexiness, yet one appears *needy* and the other doesn't.

A "Good Time Only" Woman	vs.	A "Worthwhile" Woman
She talks a lot about sex on the first date or in the first phone conversation.		She flirts more subtly and uses body language to convey her sensuality.
She wears an outfit that is very short, showing leg, cleavage, and back. Her sexuality is *overstated*. She follows the pattern of what he sees all the time.		She shows one physical attribute. Or she wears something that's slightly sheer. Her sexuality seems like it's a part of who she is. It doesn't seem forced.
She compliments him incessantly or hangs all over him.		She keeps him interested by giving him compliments when he's hoping to have sex, so he feels he's "in the game."

(continued)

A "GOOD TIME ONLY" WOMAN	VS.	A "WORTHWHILE" WOMAN
She wears a black lace teddy for him on the third date, leaving nothing for him to imagine.		She hangs the same nightie on the back of her bathroom door, so he sees it when he uses her bathroom. Then his eyes almost burn a hole through her clothes as he imagines seeing her in it.
On the second date she invites him in. He promised they'd "just cuddle." They end up sleeping together; but she ends up feeling insecure about it. He has then had the whole candy store.		They kiss passionately at the door. She'd love to invite him in, but she controls her own urges and tells him good night on her porch.
The spark fizzles.		The spark doesn't fizzle . . . it ignites.

How long should you wait before having sex? *As long as you can.* At the very least, keep it platonic for the first *month.* This tactic gives you time to learn about him. You don't want to wait until after you sleep with him to learn he's married. Or that he has an ex-girlfriend who has chronic car problems and regularly needs a lift. Or that his first cousin recently dumped him when he cheated on her with her older sister.

Giving up the candy store one jujube at a time isn't about being celibate or virginal. It is about ensuring that you look out for number one. It ensures that the man develops a habit of putting forth effort so that you are treated *the way you want to be treated.*

Not having sex right away is about playing your cards right so that small things matter. This is when he'll get a chill down his spine because you gently hold his hand in a public place. Or he'll call you several times just to get a glimpse of you. And in his mind, you are the most beautiful thing he's ever seen. It's all about having *that magic spark.* And men live for that spark.

ATTRACTION PRINCIPLE #22
Sex and the "spark" are not one and the same.

A Sweeter Victory

If a man feels as though he has to *win* you over first—sexually with his manliness, wit, or charm—he will place a higher value on you. Men are possessive. He likes knowing that other men cannot easily get to where he is trying to go. Like he's Captain Kirk and Christopher Columbus all wrapped up in one, he wants to explore new terrain not trampled on by too many men before him. And he judges whether you make "the rounds" by one thing and one thing only: how quickly you give it up to him.

It is true that there are those rare "chance" liaisons between two people who are generally not promiscuous, and it ends up working out well. But this is the exception, not the rule.

One of my closest girlfriends, Brittany, is a pharmacist and a beautiful "worthwhile" woman with a lot going for her. Almost always, she sleeps with a man on the first couple of dates.

Recently she slept with a guy she really liked. Right after they had sex, he appeared to be in his own thoughts. Then he looked at her and asked, "Do you do this with all the guys?" She recalled how it made her feel: "I was *mildly* insulted!"

If you have sex immediately with a man, he'll say to himself, for a short while, "She just couldn't resist me!" But then he'll begin to scratch his head and wonder how many *other* men you also couldn't resist.

ATTRACTION PRINCIPLE #23
Before sex, a man isn't thinking clearly and a woman is thinking clearly. After sex, it reverses. The man is thinking clearly and the woman isn't.

When sex happens at lightning speed, the man has achieved what he wanted. The reason he thinks more clearly after sex is that he's relieved and has already attained his goal. Meanwhile, the woman is just starting to pursue her goal. She has unfinished business. Then she chases *him* . . . and he runs.

Like it or not, in the beginning you're subtly negotiating the terms of your relationship. And if you strike a deal too soon, you give up all your bargaining power. The bitch takes her time deciding whether the man is someone she wants to strike a deal with in the first place. And she won't be a pit stop or a notch on a belt.

At first, he wants to sleep with you. He doesn't care what

you do for a living. He doesn't care what kind of car you drive. He doesn't care that you like a doughnut and coffee in the morning with Equal and nonfat milk. So you have to *turn it into* something else.

When you make him wait, he begins to notice that you are "different." And that's when he begins to care that you like nonfat milk, not cream, in your coffee.

ATTRACTION PRINCIPLE #24
**Every man wants to have sex *first*;
whether he wants a girlfriend is something
he thinks about *later*. By not giving him what
he wants up front, you become his girlfriend
without him realizing it.**

Men *like* the game that women find maddening. Picture the following scenario: A red-blooded American male is watching a Super Bowl game in which the score is 47 to 3. That's not very exciting, right? But if he's watching a Super Bowl game that goes into overtime—now he's on the edge of his seat for three hours. His team triumphs and he starts screaming: "Yes! Yes!" His favorite sports idol on TV is now spanking everyone else on the rear while he's breaking out the drinks for a celebration.

Ten years later, if you were to ask him about that game-winning final play, he'd describe it as though it happened yesterday. The same thing happens when a woman gives herself over slowly. He becomes much more excited about it.

This may sound "old school," but rest assured it is advice based on *countless* interviews I conducted with men, both young and old. A perfect example is Nathan. He just turned twenty-five, and he does pretty well with the ladies. Here's what he had to say, word-for-word:

> *If she gives it up too soon, we stop with the romance and we stop working at it. And truthfully, we'd rather be working hard at it. We enjoy playing the game, and if it ends too soon, we're disappointed. We even struggle inside, subconsciously. We know we want to get it, but we know we want the girl to make us wait. Otherwise, it's a one- or a two-time thing. And then you move on.*

Granted, there are some men who don't want to invest any effort. These are the men who subscribe to the "three-date rule." This rule holds that if a woman doesn't put out by the third date, the man should stop pursuing her altogether.

There are men who truly want to find a woman they can spend time with. However, the "three-date rule" is for men who have ruled out this option entirely; they just want to hit and run. If a man leaves because he didn't score by the third date, it's a clear signal he would have left after getting it anyway.

The nice girl is more likely to feel *obligated*, *pressured*, or *manipulated* to sleep with a man early on. She sleeps with him and then believes she'll hook him with great sex, as though what she has to offer sexually is "golden." The bitch understands that the sex only becomes "golden" when he doesn't get it right away.

Don't be misled by the fact that men want it quick and

they are accustomed to having it be easy. If given the option, most men would love to know how much it would take—the bottom-line dollar figure—to get a woman into bed. It's almost as if there is an *unspoken* transaction between the guy and the nice girl, in which a bartered transaction takes place: "Lookie, here. I'm willing to spend the equivalent of two dinners, a bouquet of flowers, and a movie—for a grand total of $255.92. And not a penny more."

He budgets how much he can spend and wants to know how much it will cost.

The bitch is smarter. She knows that if he's not pursuing her, he'll pursue someone else. So whatever his budget is, large or small, she makes sure it is spent on her and on no one else. In her mind, she's the best investment he'll ever make.

The "three-date rule" will fall on deaf ears with the bitch. She'll let the guy walk—and she won't barter. He will end up marrying the woman who doesn't play by his rules; she plays by her own. Since she has no problem allowing the words *See ya later* to trip lightly off her tongue, he usually doesn't feel as if he can get away with disrespecting her.

ATTRACTION PRINCIPLE #25
A man intuitively senses whether sexuality comes from a place of security or from a place of neediness. He knows when a woman is having sex to appease him.

Unlike the nice girl, the bitch believes that she has much more to offer than *just* her sexuality. So she has sex when the feeling strikes her—if and when she's comfortable with the relationship. She is plenty sexy, which is precisely why she *doesn't* throw it out there as if it's all she has.

After they consummate the relationship, this doesn't change. He is still unable to predict when he will make love to her. He doesn't know if it will happen Tuesday or Wednesday. Or Saturday or Sunday. So the mystery and the chase never go away, and he never quite feels he has fully conquered her. And that is because when she has sex with him it's *on her terms.*

When sex happens early on because the nice girl wants desperately to hold on to a man, his behavior changes completely. The dinners, the candlelight, the flowers—it all comes to a screeching halt. Instead of taking her out to dinner and a movie, now he's dropping by unannounced with a video because he already knows what's going to happen.

However, when a woman makes him wait and he's romantic over time, the dinners and the flowers keep on coming. Why? Because he formed the *habit* of treating her with respect before he got what he wanted.

ATTRACTION PRINCIPLE #26
Bad habits are easier to form than good ones, because good habits require conscious effort. Waiting encourages this effort.

A quality guy will stick around as long as he is being reassured in two areas: He wants to know that he is sexually desirable to you, and he wants to see signs that he is still in "the game." As long as he can see the light at the end of the tunnel, he'll continue to make his way down the tunnel.

However, it won't take much for him to get a mixed message or to feel he's being teased. Therefore, the next section will help you with the delicate balancing act you'll need to perform so he does not feel as though you are *teasing* him.

The Jujube Installment Plan

As you're making a concerted effort to keep the relationship out of the bedroom, remember his objective will be different than yours. You want your feet on the floor; he wants them in the air.

It's not necessarily helpful that you absolutely dig the guy and that you are *just as turned on* as he is. Giving him a mixed message will be easy, because he's ever so sexy and he's trying to seduce you. And he'll be on the lookout for any signal whatsoever that you've given him a green light. So it's important to keep the signals very clear:

- Red means no.
- Green means go.
- Yellow means you're a tease, which will piss him off.

For example, perhaps your top comes off, or there's a little bit of grinding action while you're kissing on the couch. A few minutes later, he'll think you're ready to roll. This is not the time to say, "No, I'm just not ready." Telling him this is like taking candy away from a child after you've already let him taste it.

You can't titillate him to the point of no return and then say, "No, I just don't feel right about it." He'll be thinking, "How do you not feel right about it when you're topless, you've been grinding me for an hour, and your pants are unbuttoned?"

ATTRACTION PRINCIPLE #27
If you pull the sexual plug at the last minute, he'll label you a tease.

This is where we get the term *hot and bothered*. After he's no longer hot, he will be pissed off and "bothered." He'll have far less desire to engage in the game because you've taken all the fun out of it. He no longer thinks you are playing fair, and his feelings will change from lust to *resentment*. If he feels he's being teased, he may stop pursuing you altogether.

Think about it. You can't show a dog a T-bone steak for an hour and then throw him a celery stick. If you want a man to respect you, you have to play fair.

The following guidelines will allow you to delay the time before you have sex without being perceived as a tease:

- In the beginning, try not to be alone at his place or at yours, especially very late at night.
- Do things socially that require that you to meet

somewhere in public. Or have him pick you up and then have somewhere to go.

- Do fun things during the daylight hours. If you go biking, it will seem like a red light. But if you're both wrapped up in a blanket in front of a fireplace with a bottle of wine at midnight, he'll assume you've given him a green light.

- Give kisses that are sexy and sensual. But do it while you're *out,* where it is unlikely to last too long. Don't get him worked up when you're alone together, while rolling around on the floor, a bed, or the couch.

- The first few times you go out, he may want to come in late at night, after your date. If you think he's going to make a move but you aren't quite ready, abort the mission at the door. If you live in an apartment building, say good night in the lobby. "Thanks so much, I've had a great time."

- Smile a lot, laugh at his jokes, and be good company. You want him to think of you as a friend *as well as* a lover. It's a great sign if he babbles on about himself, especially if he's a little nervous. If he likes you, he'll want to open up.

- Flirt in moderation. Be careful of sexual joking because it's never really a joke. A lot of times men will use humor to see where the parameters lie. Don't be a prude—you can laugh at the jokes and be playful. But don't stay on the subject of sex for a long time, or he'll view it as a green light.

- Compliment him. Let him know he's desirable to you. For example, lean close and smell his cologne when he gives you a hug. Or tell him he looks gorgeous. This subtly confirms you choose to wait for reasons that have nothing to do with *his* desirability.

- Show that you are affectionate and loving. Hold hands or put your head on his shoulder so he feels manly. Rub his leg lightly while you are at the movies. But don't tease him; this means stay close to the *knee*. Don't graze private areas or he'll see a green light.

- Try not to get into heavy petting in the car when he drops you off, or he'll want to get busy. Even the guy with the new BMW who makes you wipe your feet before sitting on his leather seats won't hesitate to get some "play" in his car. That's why he bought it in the first place.

- If it's late at night, don't say, "Okay, come in . . . just for a minute." Don't ask him to come in to meet your cat, Cushy. Don't offer coffee. Don't offer tea. Don't show him your remodeled place. There's no such thing as "just for a minute" after midnight.

- Don't let on you are pacing it, even though you are. Don't ever tell him he'll be waiting at least a month. Don't indicate whether he's "getting warm" and try not to give him a three-day weather forecast for predicting that you'll soon be ready. *Just don't create the opportunity for something to happen if you aren't ready to allow it to happen.*

- Don't believe him when he says, "We'll just cuddle." Even if you've known him for a long time and he's a perfect gentleman with extraordinary restraint, the objective is not to tease him.

- Be affectionate *in public*. It's generally pretty safe, because it can't go any further.

A textbook example of a sexual mixed message happened with my friend Pam. Last winter, she invited a guy to come into her home after a date because it was really cold in his car. She made hot chocolate and put on comfortable baggy flannel pajamas. They started to kiss. She assumed the flannel pajamas were so conservative that he wouldn't perceive it as an invitation to have sex. She was surprised to discover that he had much more than hot chocolate on his mind.

Bedroom clothes are *b-e-d-r-o-o-m clothes* to a man. Wearing something cozy that you sleep in (even ugly boxers or flannel sleepers) will be perceived as a green light.

Even though he'll subtly pressure you, if he really likes you, a part of him deep down will want you to make him wait. He wants to believe you are "different." He wants you to think he is neat, cool, and handsome. He wants you to laugh at his jokes and think he is funny. He wants a goddess. He wants . . . Wonder Woman.

So how do you give him this impression? Simple. Let him pursue you and don't give yourself over too easily. Throw on a pair of go-go boots and suddenly you become the Wonder Woman of his dreams.

The Sweet Spot

When a man and a woman become lovers, there are still behaviors that differentiate the doormat and the dreamgirl.

One of the biggest mistakes the nice girl makes is she competes with other women. She may ask him about another woman in the room, "Is she pretty?" Or, she may be competing with whatever she *thinks* he fantasizes about: a model, a centerfold, a stripper, or a porn star.

ATTRACTION PRINCIPLE #28
If he makes you feel insecure, let your insecurity be your guide.

It's often said that a woman doesn't reach her sexual peak until after she turns thirty. It takes a lot of women until then to overcome their insecurity or the feeling that they have to compete with other women. Sex becomes better because she can tell him what she likes. She's more secure. She's more assertive. She can let go because she is not self-conscious.

A lot of women feel pressured to live up to an ideal. Or they feel that in the bedroom they have to put on a riveting performance. I've even heard some men critique women and say, "The louder she screams, the better."

A look at how widespread pornography has become only confirms how unrealistic the standards have become. Even porn movies utilize fake "voiceovers." This means that the girl screaming, "Yes! Yes! Give it to me, yes!" is often a fully dressed 400-pound woman who is sitting on a stool in a studio and screaming into a microphone.

The bitch doesn't usually define herself by outside standards. But often, women who are *too* nice are *too* busy trying to measure up. When a woman is *too* concerned with performance issues in bed, she completely forgets why she's there in the first place. It's not sex; it's "animation" time.

How to Fake an Orgasm— The Animated Guide

- Arch your back at a 45-degree angle and pant like a dog.

- Recite a couple of bad lines from a B-rated blue movie. Example: Tell Big Poppa he does it for you like no one else can.

- And the basics: "**Yes, yes, yes . . . harder, harder** . . . **don't stop**!" Then you'll want to immediately slap the nearest pillow.

- Mix it up. This means sometimes you'll want to slap the pillow then scream, other times you want to scream first, then slap the pillow. Men love variety.

- Don't forget to suck your finger.

- Now for show and tell: Ask him whose "it" is, and tell him that it's his!

- If he switches positions, stops for a rest, or reaches for a drink of water, pay no attention and keep screaming anyway.

- Now for the alleged orgasm: Scream like a banshee, and begin those Kegel exercises. Squeeze . . . release . . . squeeze . . . release.

- And after sex, don't forget pillow talk. You've had two men before him. (Okay, three, tops. But that's your final offer.)

WARNING: If your man sees this page, it could have an adverse effect (erectile dysfunction).

A bitch is far less likely to put on a "cartoon" show. She is much more honest. She asks for what she wants. If he doesn't do it right, she *won't* encourage him by giving disingenuous feedback. Yet then he doesn't learn how to please her, and that won't work because the bitch rightly cares about her own pleasure.

I don't recommend that a woman fake an orgasm. This little lesson is a satire on the pressures women feel to perform. If a man makes you feel as though you are on stage competing in a pageant, don't sleep with him.

It is much more of a turn-on to a man when a woman is able to be herself and she's honest about what she likes and dislikes. A man loves watching his woman being pleased by him; it's an automatic turn-on. And that's much more important than putting on an award-winning performance.

ATTRACTION PRINCIPLE #29
A quality guy fantasizes about a woman who genuinely loves sex.

Half of pleasing him is getting off yourself, not faking it. It's true that a man's ego has to be stroked and properly dealt with, but that's what *your* satisfaction accomplishes. The same principle that holds true outside the bedroom holds true inside the bedroom: The bitch can better please him because she is more concerned with pleasing herself. He knows without question that she loves every minute of it. And this feeds his ego like nothing else can.

The nice girl will also make the mistake of being disingenuous in other ways. For example, suppose she sleeps with him on the second date and he asks how many lovers she's had. She gives the oldest line in the book: "I've only had three lovers."

The bitch will not go there. She won't sleep with a guy right away and then try to give the almost-virgin shtick: "I've only had three lovers . . . the first one hurt . . . the second wasn't as good as you . . . the third one had three inches and thirty seconds of fury . . . and the fourth . . . uh, oops . . . there wasn't a fourth. Okay, yes, there was a fourth. But we didn't go all the way, so it doesn't count . . . the fifth one doesn't matter either because I was drunk . . . ."

If you tell him you've had three lovers and you are over the age of a fetus, he'll know you're a straight-up liar. Show him with your actions that you are a classy woman by letting him wait. And if he pries or wants to know about your private life say, "I probably haven't been with as many men as you've been with women." If you become defensive as if you have something to hide, up goes the red flag.

What do you do when he boasts about his past conquests? The *last* thing you want to do is listen, because you'll get the embellished version—and you might actually believe some of it is true.

The bitch is the woman who will look at her watch in an effort to drop a hint when he brings up another woman. She already knows what she has to offer is enough—take it or leave it. And if he doesn't change the subject by the time she's done winding her watch, she will. "Honey, I'm not one of the guys. Please don't tell me about other women you've been with."

ATTRACTION PRINCIPLE #30
**Any time a woman competes with
another woman, she demeans herself.**

Remember, inside the bedroom as well as outside the bedroom, men are used to women who are insecure, which is all the more reason to be different. You need to exude the attitude that you are confident and that you aren't concerned with whether you measure up or whether another woman can steal him away.

If the subject of other women comes up, casually throw this into one of your conversations: "If any woman can steal a guy away from me, then she can have him because I wouldn't want him anymore." Then smile, take a sip of your wine, and change the subject. "Seen any good movies lately?"

If you don't trust him, stop seeing him. But until he gives you a reason not to trust him, behave as though you trust him. It will make you look secure with yourself as if you are saying with your actions, "Well, *of course,* you want to be with me!"

ATTRACTION PRINCIPLE #31
**When there is that undeniable "spark,"
there is only one key to the lock.**

A quality guy wants to feel trusted because it makes him feel as though you believe in his character. Until he gives you a reason not to trust him, trust him. If he's falling in love with you, he won't tell you he wants to be with you exclusively—you'll automatically know. He'll be calling you every day and he will insist that you date only him. Because he won't want anyone else coming near his *dreamgirl*.

4

Dumb

LIKE A FOX

How to Convince Him He's in Control While You Run the Show

> " I have an idea that the phrase 'weaker sex' was coined by some woman to disarm the man she was preparing to overwhelm. "
>
> —OGDEN NASH

The Dumb Fox Handles His Ego with Kid Gloves

In the last chapter we touched on why power is intoxicating to a man in the very same way that romance is intoxicating to a woman. And now . . . a closer look.

In order to motivate a man to give, he must feel good when he gives. He wants to feel appreciated and revered. Ego is the reason men go to war. It's the reason they build large corporations. Ego is the reason they stick needles in their butts at the gym before lifting heavy weights. It's the reason they beg, steal, and borrow. And ego is the reason they fall in love.

The explanation may sound obvious, but it's not: A man needs to feel "manly." That's why he won't stop to ask for directions. It doesn't matter if you tell him that six exits ago he was supposed to go west. He'll still push the pedal to the metal and hightail it in the opposite direction. Men don't get lost. They merely . . .

- "Get familiar with another area."
- "Change destinations."
- "Look to see what is down another street."
- "Explore new terrain."

He's never lost. No, Inspector Gadget is merely "checking things out" in every last square foot of a 37-mile radius that is outside the intended destination.

If you want him to turn right, tell him "I think it might be to the left." In a man's mind, his navigation skills will always be superior to a woman's. It's all about his ego, which has no direction and no line of rotation.

The three words guaranteed to turn any man on? "You are right." You'll never convince him otherwise, so don't bother trying.

Let him be *right*. You be *smart*. This is precisely the reason the dumb fox lets a man think he's in control. When you appeal to his feeling of power, you "charge up his batteries." Then you're giving him what he needs and he *doesn't even know it*.

ATTRACTION PRINCIPLE #32
Let him think he's in control. He'll automatically start doing things you want done because he'll always want to look like "a king" in your eyes.

A couple of times a week when he's kind or generous, let him know he's the top dog. Make him feel as though he's the alpha-dog and the Grand Poo-Bah. He wears the pants, and he is the man. Meanwhile, guess who is getting her way?

My friend Annette learned this the hard way. She made the mistake of telling her new boyfriend about how she had killed a snake in her backyard. He asked her, "How in the world did you kill it?" She went on in detail about how she used a very large shovel to "do battle." A look of complete and utter horror came over his face as she gave him a graphic play-by-play of the brutal "massacre." Later that night, he couldn't get an erection.

An obvious "penile" code infraction: When you act too much like Tarzan, he feels too much like Jane. Don't even kill a bug when he's around. Don't change a tire. In fact, don't even change a light bulb. (Heaven forbid, sister.)

For any red-blooded male, the feeling that he is the "man" is the ticket. This doesn't mean that you should be docile all the time. At the same time that you show him you offer him "a mental challenge," remember that he needs to have his ego stroked. There is a very big difference between catering to his ego and appearing *needy*. You shouldn't show that you "need" him to help you with:

- Common sense
- Coping with everyday life
- Emotional stability
- Reassurance of your self-worth
- Self-esteem
- Feeling complete as a person

These things signify *neediness*. However, you *can* show that you need and appreciate his *masculinity*. He'll absolutely eat out of your hand when he feels that you like his "manliness" or that you admire his . . . brawn.

ATTRACTION PRINCIPLE #33
When you cater to his ego in a soft way, he doesn't try to get power in an aggressive way.

Praise is an effective tool in getting him to treat you the way you want. Don't complain, "Well, you *used* to bring me flowers." From this point forward, every bouquet he gives you is the "prettiest you have ever seen." Don't complain that he doesn't take you out enough. Instead, every restaurant he takes you to is "unbelievable" or "amazing."

When he asks if you've been to the restaurant before, don't tell him about the two ex-boyfriends who took you to the very same romantic corner table you are now sitting at. (Unless you never want to go back to that restaurant again.)

ATTRACTION PRINCIPLE #34
When you appear softer and more feminine, you appeal to his instinct to *protect*. When you appear more aggressive, you appeal to his instinct to *compete*.

Whenever you give a man the impression that you want to "wear the pants," you'll almost always have a battle on your hands, in which case, congrats—you've become his opponent. If he competes, he plays to win at your expense, and good luck getting anything that way.

Men need a little coaching, and the way to coach them is to praise them when they behave well. A man's favorite word? "Best." It doesn't matter if you say, "Honey, you eat those beer nuts the best—like no one I have ever met in my life." Use the word *best,* and you'll always have his full attention.

Make friends with his ego. For example, suppose you live together and he wants to help decorate. Chances are at some point he will have a need to "express" his virility by hanging something on the wall. (Something that clashes with *everything*.) When he gleefully breaks out those elephant tusks, the African sword, or the 1986 Super Bowl poster that he calls "art," keep a straight face and appear sincere. "Yes, honey, Grandpa's eighteenth-century rifle is to die for!" Then immediately enlist his "much needed help" in decorating the garage or the basement.

Want him to pitch in around the house? Just make him feel needed (i.e., powerful). Give him little assignments. It doesn't matter if you ask him to program the VCR or help hang a photo on the wall. When he uses that noisy electric drill, he will feel just like Rambo. When the picture hangs crooked—and it will—pretend it's perfect. Simply wait until he leaves the room and then straighten it.

When he hands over that paycheck, thank him for working so hard for "the benefit of everyone in the family." Again, wait until he leaves the room. Then review the stub to make sure that he got paid all of his overtime.

Remember, when he behaves like a man and he treats you well, pay a little "homage" to that ego. He should feel like Conan the Barbarian a couple of times a week.

Whenever he does something handy around the house like putting up a shelf, praise him. It doesn't matter if the shelf hangs at a 45-degree angle and the stuff keeps sliding off the other end. Clap like the happiest seal at the zoo, and then have a handyman come over to fix it when he isn't around. The minute you say, "It's crooked," it's all over. He'll never do anything handy around the house again. It will make him feel worse than a little kid who got scolded in arts and crafts class.

Men have big egos and they need to have them stroked. This is what the "dumb fox" does. In small ways, she makes him feel like he is the King Kong of her world. Here are a few more dumb fox tips on how to make him feel "studly."

- If you're walking your dog at dusk, ask him to come with you because you want him to "keep you safe."
- If he kills a little bug, look away. And don't turn back around until he lets you know he has "secured the premises."
- If you hear a noise at night (like a bird pooping on the roof), act really scared. Tell him to check to see "what that noise is about."
- After he checks out the source of the noise, tell him you like having him in the house or apartment because it makes you "feel so much safer."
- Ask him to open a jar that you can't open (even if you can) or unzip your dress (even if you can reach it). Or, you can ask him to lift a small box for you.
- At a scary movie, hang on to him tightly. If there's violence, cover your eyes and let him tell you when it's over.
- If it's cold outside, crawl under his coat and hang on to him for warmth.
- Let him move a piece of furniture (even one you could move yourself). When he does this with ease, tell him how heavy it was. "You are so strong! Gee, I don't know how you moved that."
- Let him parallel park your car or back it out of a tight

spot. If you tell him he's a "much better driver" than you are, he'll really be eating out of your hand. He'll probably wash your car or fill your tank with gas.

Handling his ego with kid gloves is as easy as learning your *A-B-Cs*. When her child brings home a crayon drawing from kindergarten—no matter how ugly it is—a mother doesn't criticize it. She'd never say, "Is that a dog or a cow? Hey kid—don't quit your day job." Instead she tells him, "This is a masterpiece!" Then the child thinks he is the next Picasso, and he draws ten more pictures.

Praise is important. When he takes you out to eat, say thank-you *once* at dinner, and again when you say good night. The nice girl often makes the mistake of saying thank-you over and over. Then she calls the following day to say thank-you three times on his answering machine. As though no one's ever bought her a hot meal before.

In the beginning, without question let *him* pay for dinner. After you've been dating for a while, you can reciprocate. But don't do a 50/50 split or go Dutch—he's not a long-lost professional colleague.

When a man is really crazy about a woman, he isn't concerned with splitting a check. He won't say, "You had the turkey salad and I had the beef. So your total comes to…" If he adores her, he won't be thinking about petty cash. What he'll be thinking about is how he can win her over.

If he can't afford it, suggest an inexpensive place or do something that doesn't cost money. Visit a museum. Go on a bike ride. Split a dinner plate, and don't order alcohol. However, if he asks you to split the check on the first few dates, don't see him again. It has less to do with a few dollars than with the fact that he's not very concerned with impressing you. And that's never a good sign.

ATTRACTION PRINCIPLE #35
He'll let a woman who becomes his doormat pay for dinner on the first couple of dates, but he wouldn't *think* of it with his *dreamgirl*.

This conversation came up on my radio show. A caller asked if she should let the man pay, and I said, "In the beginning, *yes*." Both my male guest and the male sound engineer jumped in and said, "But that's not fair." Then I got a spelling lesson: "Fair. It's spelled *f-a-i-r.*" I see their point. But it also isn't fair that we get sixty cents on the dollar in the workplace, that we wear painful pushup bras and high heels, and that we carry the babies and give birth. So let him be the man. A *gentle*man.

The important thing is that when he pays, let him know at the end of the dinner you *really do appreciate it*. And compliment him on his taste in food, wine, or the restaurant. If it wasn't good, don't comment.

The dumb fox knows that the less she criticizes, the better. Which is why she doesn't nag. Instead, she *maneuvers*.

For example, when he leaves his clothes on the floor next to the bed before he turns in for the night . . . don't worry about it. He'll probably get out of bed in the morning and pick them up. And then he'll put them right back on.

About those socks and underwear that are peppered

throughout your home? That was your fault, because you bought a hamper *with* a lid. (Much too complicated.) Get a hamper with no lid and strategically put it in a corner. Congrats. You've erected your very own basketball hoop. Every time he makes a dunk shot out of his dirty underwear? Two points.

Do you always change the toilet paper roll? Does he always get a full roll, while you get the last crummy little square, half of which is stuck to the cardboard? Nothing a little housebreaking won't fix.

One Sunday morning, he'll go in the bathroom and take his seat with the sports section. He won't notice the absence of toilet paper for twenty minutes because he'll be fixated on the stats from Saturday's football game. Then, when he's finished reading he'll call, "Honey? Honey?! Can you hear me?!" (No response.)

This is your cue to take out the kitchen trash. After all, the sun is shining, the flowers are blooming, and the birds are chirping. (Trivia question: How long before he realizes there's more toilet paper under the sink?)

If he doesn't help out around the house, the dumb fox doesn't complain and say, "You can't put a price on what I do around the house." Instead, she gets an estimate from a maid service. See how easy? Now not only does she "put a price on it," she even pays it to someone *else*.

Here's another example of how a dumb fox might "maneuver." A friend named Sharon was running herself ragged trying to clean up after her kids and her husband. She wanted to have someone come in to help her once a week. Her husband was very opposed to paying $50 for a maid every week, even though they could afford it. He kept insisting on "just once a month."

Sharon played the dumb fox and agreed to a maid once a month—sort of. She wrote a check to the maid once a month, and each of the other three weeks she asked for $50 in cash back when she wrote a check at the market. Not only did this prevent weekly arguments, he came home to a beautifully cleaned house every week.

The Dumb Fox Credo as outlined here, allows for smooth sailing and no room for conflict:

- Agree with everything.
- Explain nothing.
- Then do what is best for you. It will make life a whole lot easier.

For example, the dumb fox is smart enough to save herself the grief by insisting on separate bathrooms. First of all, the concept of guest towels or decorative towels is foreign to men. To him, a towel is a towel, which means a bath towel is a beach towel is a car-wash towel is an oil-changing towel. You would think he'd "spare" the pretty one with the pink bow, but no such luck. And the towels you use on your face? Say hello to your new floor mop.

Once in a while, you'll come across a man who is extra clean. But generally, sharing a bathroom with a man will be sheer misery. Ten minutes after you've cleaned the sink and mirror with streak-free Windex, he'll come in there and spray water everywhere. It's like sharing a bathroom with your very own, in-house, adopted walrus. Scientists have not yet joined with zoologists to do a study on why it is that men "spray." So, until they figure it out, insist that you have your own bathroom.

The dumb fox also cleverly divides up the personal space in the home with the utmost fairness. She gives him 20 percent of the closet, but "the whole garage" or basement to himself. He also controls the lawnmower, the cars, the barbecue, and the tools. Remember: Men are very territorial, so you'll also want to designate the yard as his domain in the "habitat." It will come in handy when you're hogging the bathroom.

In Japan, there is an interesting motto: A smart eagle does not show her claws. American women perceive Japanese women as submissive because they bow to men and walk behind them in the streets. However, Japanese men typically bring their paychecks home and give them to their wives. *The wife controls the purse strings in the Japanese home and decides how the money is spent.*

Now we uncover the *real* reason why a Japanese woman may walk behind her man in the street: It is those deep, heavy pockets that are slowing her down. The poor thing can hardly keep up.

In addition to having to feel he's "right," a man needs to have things be "his idea." So, remember, it's *always* his idea. Even if it *isn't*, convince him that it is.

When you're in front of a group of friends and he steps in and takes credit for something that you thought of, don't make a fuss over it. He needs to show that he's the chief. Don't correct him or try to "show him up" in front of your mutual friends because he'll feel emasculated. It's like a mommy scolding her little boy in front of his friends at school. Publicly, he needs to "save face."

If it's absolutely necessary, wait until you are alone with him to bring up something he did that may have bothered you. Address it *privately,* not in front of people. If it's unimportant nonsense, let him take all the credit. Who cares? The dumb fox knows better. She never starts a fight over something trivial, particularly if she knows in advance she'll gain absolutely nothing from winning. The dumb fox is strong in a demure way. She stands her ground, but she's not a ball-buster. She employs the "Science of Compliance." She appears to give up power, but gains leverage in the process.

ATTRACTION PRINCIPLE #36
**The token power position is for public display,
but the true power position is for private viewing only.
And this is the only one that matters.**

For all "ego-intensive" purposes, help him look manly in front of other people. Let him open doors and let him address the hostess at the restaurant. "Johnson. Party of 4." This is just the *token* power position which is meaningless.

When you are truly running the show, you don't need to tip your hand or flaunt it. If he is treating you like you are his dreamgirl, you have all the power you need. Remember, feminine strength is equally as powerful. It's poetic justice: Men control the world, but women control the men.

Alice, an attractive older woman who has been married for many years, shared the following advice. "Whenever I want to do something, I convince my husband it was his idea. I'll say 'Sweetie, would you like to go to this restaurant or that one?' He's paying, so I always let him think he's the one choosing. And after we're done eating? I tell him, 'What a great idea that was!'"

Most men know it's a turn-on to a woman if they do romantic things, but women don't understand that giving men the feeling of power has the same effect. It melts them like butter. It is a good-natured way of gaining leverage in your relationship.

Men do the very same thing. They know that we like roses. If they never saw another rose, it would be no loss to them. They're as attached to the roses as they are to a plant in their office building or a weed growing in the cracks of a sidewalk.

Most women generally won't say no to any reasonable request made by a man who has just brought a beautiful bouquet of roses. When you appeal to his ego, it has the same effect. He'll want to remain a king in your eyes, and he'll want to please you. Men work their whole lives just to have a woman look at them adoringly and say, "You're wonderful" and "I admire you." He'll climb a whole mountain just to feel admired by a woman he loves.

ATTRACTION PRINCIPLE #37
If you give him a feeling of power, he'll want to protect you and he'll want to give you the world.

Once you're in charge of that relationship, you're giving him what he needs (power) and he *doesn't even know it*. It works with even the smartest men. Here's what Albert Einstein said about his wife on their fiftieth wedding anniversary:

> *When we first got married, we made a pact. It was this: In our life together, it was decided I would make all of the big decisions and my wife would make all of the little decisions. For fifty years, we have held true to that agreement. I believe that is the reason for the success in our marriage. However, the strange thing is that in fifty years, there hasn't been one big decision.*

The dumb fox doesn't have to "obey" her man as in, "I promise to love, honor, and *obey* until death do us part." She has her own rendition of the marital vows. She "promises to love, honor, and *appear to be agreeable some of the time.*"

This is not a lesson in how to give up your power or become more docile. This is a lesson in how to gain power because you appeal to a man and make him channel his energies *toward you.* Men need a little help when it comes to emotions, because they aren't always aware of what motivates them. You have to make him think he's in charge; then he'll be much more attuned to what you need and he'll apply much more effort to please you. It keeps him stimulated and it keeps his interest. Then he wants to give you the reins; at which point, you will have all the power that you need.

The Dumb Fox Is a Clever Negotiator

Now that women are long established in the work force, men don't feel they're *needed* as much. Even though they work as hard, they don't get the feeling of being appreciated as the "man of the house" as much as they used to. As Erica Jong said, "Beware of the man who praises women's liberation. He's about to quit his job."

Women who are successful in other areas of life are often the ones who find themselves saying, "I should not have to apologize for being strong." Then the following week they wonder why they "can't find a good man." Because a good man wants a good *w-o-m-a-n*. Being a bitch does not mean you lose your femininity. And it also doesn't mean you overtly try to wear the pants in the house. It just means you don't allow anyone to walk all over you.

The classic superwoman wants a relationship in which the man and woman are "equals." This is a nice theory, but in practice it becomes a one-sided relationship pretty quickly.

ATTRACTION PRINCIPLE #38
**When a woman acts as though she's capable
of everything, she gets stuck doing everything.**

For this reason, be careful how you set the tone in the beginning. Never start what you don't want to continue. If you don't want to cook every night, don't start out cooking every night. If you don't want to go to the grocery store all the time, don't set the pattern of doing it all the time. Let him come your way.

In the beginning, men are so willing to make an impression, and this is why they are especially accommodating. This is precisely when you'll want to help him form good habits.

Later, when everything has been done for him, he'll be too set in his ways to change.

For example, after a few dates you may find yourself standing under the arch of your front door, kissing him good night. It's a moment to behold. The stars are twinkling, the moonlight is breathtaking, and you both look up to find a shooting star. He'll barely notice your kitchen trash is under his left arm.

If a man offers to take you to lunch or dinner, let him. If he asks if he can bring over takeout, bring on the egg rolls. If he asks to get you something from the grocery store, let him pick up sorbet in the flavor you like. It isn't about him paying the three dollars. It makes him happy to feel he's meeting your needs. And it makes him feel as if he's "driving that train." Even though you really are.

The hardest lesson for the nice girl to learn is how to receive. Let him give to you, because part of his manhood is defined by feeling "responsible."

The dumb fox doesn't give up power, she simply creates the appearance that she does. And this very much helps her positioning power because she gets what she wants.

Here's a classic example. A woman I know named Michelle told me about a man she's seeing. On the second date, he asked her if she'd drive to his place. She was put on the spot and then pulled a dumb fox move. She ignored the request and very sweetly asked, "Would you prefer to get together another night? If tonight is inconvenient, I do understand."

Michelle averted the question completely. She didn't act upset or tell him what to do. She simply gave him a couple of alternatives, one of which is that she may not participate.

Then she let *him* choose.

The beauty is that the dumb fox is agreeable, tactful, and always polite, so he thinks he's in control (even though he isn't). Even though the dumb fox *appears* oblivious, she is very aware. It's no different than a successful business negotiation:

1. She doesn't spell out where she's coming from.
2. She's prepared to walk away, if the terms aren't favorable to her.

The dumb fox does both, without words. She negotiates with her willingness (or lack thereof) to participate. If the offer sounds good, she says, "I'd love to." If the offer doesn't sound good, she answers, "I'd love to, but I'm pooped." She responds favorably when he behaves like a gentleman and backs off in a subtle way if his manners fall short.

ATTRACTION PRINCIPLE #39
**Men don't respond to words.
They respond to no contact.**

Being dumb like a fox can also defuse a situation in which he is slightly disrespectful. For example, let's say you're waiting to be seated for dinner on your first date, and he puts his hand on your lower back—*very* low on your back—as in, any lower and he knows whether you prefer to wear a brief or a thong. All you need to do is play dumb, step aside as if it were a complete accident, and say, "Oops, excuse me."

Another example happened with my friend Talia. She was at dinner and the waiter brought the check to the table. Her date made a joke to the waiter about giving the bill to her and then looked at her to get her reaction. She titled her head sideways and looked confused as if to suggest that she's never heard anything like this before. Then she started to blink as though she might have been hallucinating.

The dumb fox doesn't spell things out. The nice girl, on the other hand, makes the mistake of wearing her heart on her sleeve almost all the time. As one man named Paul said, "Women talk too much. If she's upset, she'll go on and on. I'd rather get into a ring with Mike Tyson for six rounds than hear a woman repeat herself over and over."

Think about the last time a man spilled his guts. At first it feels like "bonding." But the novelty wears off very quickly. Men want bonding, sure—*below* the waist.

The two-hour phone calls you love are a big mistake. He likes it the first time because he knows you're interested. After that, he *hates* it. Don't let conversations on the phone last too long. Don't let yourself be perceived as a tiresome *obligation*. Keep the phone calls short and sweet—and he'll never get tired of calling.

ATTRACTION PRINCIPLE #40
Talking about the "relationship" too much takes away the element of the "unknown" and thus the mystery.

When you aren't needy, you don't require a play-by-play from the sidelines about the relationship. When you are secure with yourself, he *doesn't feel he has a 100 percent hold on you*. And when he doesn't have a 100 percent hold on you, he eats out of your hand.

Eliminate the following words from your vocabulary: *We need to talk.* My friend Jeanette shared her observations on men with me: "You have to sneak up on them. Feed them, get them a beer, and then casually bring it up. Go through the back door. In and out—before they realize what has happened."

When men talk to each other, they say their piece and then the other one responds. One nods. The other grunts. One takes a shot; the other buys him a beer. The most feed-back he'll get is a couple of sentences. Did you blink? The "bonding" has commenced.

Most men have a concentration threshold for the "mushy" stuff that lasts about two minutes. Right around the second minute, his mind will start to wander. He'll be thinking, "Man, I'm getting hungry. I wonder what we're having for dinner?"

ATTRACTION PRINCIPLE #41
**Men respect women who communicate
in a succinct way, because it's the language
men use to talk to one another.**

The bitch communicates differently from the nice girl. A bitch tells it like it is in a matter-of-fact way and gets her point across succinctly. The nice girl wears her heart on her sleeve and pours out her guts. And what does he hear? Nothing at all. However, he does see her neediness, which eventually turns him off.

The Dumb Fox Is More Mysterious

The dumb fox knows that familiarity breeds contempt, so she doesn't spill her guts on the first couple of dates. She lets the "cream rise to the top" without rushing things.

When you first meet a man, don't overcompensate by doing all the talking. Don't talk constantly *out of nervousness*. Keeping cool and quiet will give you more appeal, not to mention the ability to wield more power.

I was once on a date with a man I had just met. He began to share all the sordid details of his last relationship. I had no desire to listen, but I didn't criticize him or make him feel "wrong." I was polite. I simply asked, "So John, what's your workload like at the office this week?"

The dumb fox does *not* ask, "May we change the subject?" Permission isn't necessary.

The dumb fox also doesn't tell him about her past relationships. You're "a prize," and you don't have a long list of calamities to report. He doesn't need to know that your ex-husband stole your appliances, is defaulting on his child support, and has a Mafioso brother who is doing time for racketeering. If he's classy, he won't be impressed that your last boyfriend is "still stalking you and can't let go."

If he asks about your ex, you say, "We went our separate ways." Here's another option: "We wanted different things."

The dumb fox relies on a "vague generality" when he asks for information that's none of his business.

As far as what *you* disclose? Don't volunteer bad information about yourself. He doesn't need to know that you're insecure about your thighs or that you haven't been on a date in 7.2 months. Inquiring minds do *not* need to know.

Men automatically assume that, if you're interested, you'll do anything to "nail him down." He immediately thinks you want "exclusivity"; you want to break open the hope chest and have babies with him. It's important for him to think you're different: You are relaxed, secure, and happy *with him* or *without him*. This is known as the happy-go-lucky formula, described in Attraction Principle #42.

ATTRACTION PRINCIPLE #42
When you are always HAPPY;

And he is always free to GO;

He feels LUCKY.

If you want to talk about your favorite ice cream, go for it. Traveling to Belize? Yes. Your problems at work or your disappointing visit to the fertility doctor? No.

It's perfectly okay to leave some of his questions about you *unanswered*. In fact, it is advisable to do so. When all is said and done, a person shows you who he or she is. No one will come out and tell you. Therefore, what a person shows you with actions is the *only* language that matters.

The Dumb Fox Is True to Herself

The fox is the smaller animal, and in the animal kingdom, the smaller animal is the prey. Therefore, the fox knows it is incumbent on her to look out for her own best interests, especially in the beginning of a relationship. On the other hand, the nice girl believes everything she's told because it sounds good, which puts her out there to get hurt. The fox knows that, in the beginning, a man is likely to "flower up" his intentions; therefore, she must stay alert.

What He *Won't* Say	What He *Will* Say
"I want sex and only sex, with no strings attached."	"I'm interested in having a long-term relationship!"
"Give me sex, and I'll pretend to be your boyfriend for a week."	"Trust me."
"Hey, can I rotate you with three other women, like a pitching staff?"	"You are so different."
"Wanna be the flavor of the month?"	"I am so tired of the dating scene."

Trivia question: Which guy scores more women: the guy who "flowers up" his intentions, or the guy who tells it like it is? The point is, if he has a hidden agenda the last thing he'll do is spell it out for her. So it's up to the fox to figure things out on her own.

The reason the dumb fox doesn't reveal what she observes is that he'll show his true colors much more quickly when he doesn't realize he is being watched. When a man talks about himself or past relationships, he may do so as a way of helping her "get to know him." Rather than getting into heavy question-and-answer sessions, the fox keeps the conversation light. Why? The truest things are said in jest. He'll tell you everything you need to know in passing conversation, with a joke or an off-the-cuff remark here and there. If he's a wolf dressed up as a sheep, his whiskers will inevitably pop out.

When the dumb fox senses something's "just not right" with a man's character, she does *not* bring it to his attention. The only conversation the dumb fox has is *between her two ears.* As President Lyndon B. Johnson said, "You've got to know when to keep your mouth shut."

When you tell someone who may be manipulating you what you observe, he will immediately try to talk you out of it. He'll say, "You're insecure" or "You're prejudging me." Are you prejudging him? You had *better* be. The only mistake is letting him know it.

The dumb fox is self-reliant. She judges people by her own experiences. The dumb fox takes better care of herself and makes better choices because she lets time elapse and she watches to see how the man *behaves.* She trusts her observations and she trusts her animal instincts.

No hunted animal gives the "benefit of the doubt." The fox senses danger and hightails it out of there. Never be around a person who has shown you he is a hurtful person. If he does this by accident, that's one thing. But if he's hurtful on purpose? Game over. You've learned everything you need to know.

In the beginning, have fun and go out . . . but keep your cards close to your vest. Most important, *take your time.* This will not only make you smart as a fox, it will help you keep your independence.

The nice girl loses an important protective mechanism when she assumes that life is fair, or that Prince Charming will always protect her. The smart fox is not governed by wishful thinking or the hope of a fantasy outcome, like Cinderella. Despite appearances, she trusts herself to watch her *own* back instead of giving a man the responsibility of doing it for her.

It's what every animal in the wild does to survive, so that they don't become "din din." Above all, the smart fox understands—and adheres to—the first law of nature: Every animal for herself.

5

JUMPING THROUGH *Hoops* LIKE A CIRCUS POODLE

When Women Give Themselves Away and Become Needy

> " Let us never negotiate out of fear. "
>
> —JOHN F. KENNEDY

A New School: Who Is the Boss of You?

When a nice girl meets a man, it's not uncommon for her to make concessions in her life that seem relatively insignificant. She stops doing the routine everyday things. She stops seeing friends. She stops going to a yoga class, and she stops playing tennis on weekends. She stops making time for the things she did when she was "solo." Here's what she *does* do:

- She cancels a hair appointment . . . for a date with *him*.
- She stops going to the gym after work . . . to accommodate seeing *him*.
- She stops spending time with friends . . . to give *him* the feeling "he is special."
- She cancels plans . . . because there's a chance that she'll get a call from *him*.
- She isn't focused at school . . . she keeps checking to see if a message came from *him*.
- She isn't focused at work . . . she keeps checking her e-mail to see if she received something in her inbox from *him*.
- She gives up her career . . . to further his career and support *him*.
- She stops having dreams outside of her relationship . . . because her only dream is *him*.

The bitch does not stop *moving to her own rhythm*. This, in and of itself, prevents her from becoming off-balance like a nice girl who abandons her routine.

ATTRACTION PRINCIPLE #43
If you allow your rhythm to be interrupted, you'll create a void. Then, to replace what you give up, you'll start to expect and need more from your partner.

A classic example is Theresa. She takes salsa dance classes two nights a week. When she met her last boyfriend, she stopped going to her dance classes because he didn't like to dance. She also played tennis, but he didn't play; so she stopped that hobby as well.

Seems harmless, right? Not really. She's giving up what she likes. The reason the nice girl gives up these activities is also telling of her self-confidence. Often she gives up something because she fears he won't like her the way she is.

In addition, this cumulative reduction of activities eventually adds up to a significant change in *who* she is. At some point the man notices, and it turns him off because he realizes—before she does—that she's lost her independence.

What happens after she's lost her independence? Let's take a look at the "state of the union" with Theresa, the woman who gave up salsa classes and tennis. She said, "We spent almost every night of the week together and fell into that pattern almost immediately. He didn't tell me it was 'too much' for him. He just didn't smile much and it seemed like he wasn't happy anymore. I was becoming more insecure and I kept trying harder to be affectionate. I just wanted him to be like he was in the beginning."

ATTRACTION PRINCIPLE #44
Most women are starving to receive something from a man that they need to give to themselves.

The nice girl thinks she's giving up something to get something *better* in return. She gives up control over her own life. When the time comes for her to get what she had expected, she winds up disappointed. In addition to being empty-handed, she's depleted.

A man rarely realizes just how much the nice girl gives up. He doesn't make the same sacrifices because she's adjusting her life to be with him. After she gives up everything in her life, she begins to demand the same of him. She wants him to stop seeing family and friends. She wants him to spend all of his free time with her. If he goes to the gym, she wants to accompany him.

He doesn't feel this pressure from a bitchier woman, so he wants to be around her more, not less, and he respects her because she appears to have "a life." Suppose a woman says to a guy she can't go on a date with him that night because of her weekly pottery class. He scratches his head and thinks, "She'd rather go to a pottery class than be with me?" It not only attracts him; it blows his mind.

ATTRACTION PRINCIPLE #45
A woman looks more secure in a man's eyes when he can't pull her away from her life, because she is *content* with her life.

When you love life *with him* or *without him*, that is when he will accept and value you for who you are.

WHO IS THE BOSS OF YOU?

THE NICE GIRL	THE BITCH
The nice girl dismisses what she used to value and what used to be important in her life.	The bitch values her priorities, her values, and her preferences. Always.
He is the boss . . . of her.	She stays the boss . . . of herself.
The nice girl searches for a sign from him to see when the closeness is "too much."	The bitch acts as her own guide. She doesn't allow him an opportunity to be bored.
He is the boss . . . of her.	She stays the boss . . . of herself.
The nice girl senses how happy he is, paying close attention to his approval of her.	The bitch doesn't obsess over his opinion or need his approval.
He is the boss . . . of her.	She stays the boss . . . of herself.

(continued)

THE NICE GIRL	THE BITCH
When he's "into it" with the nice girl, she feels good; when he snubs her, she feels bad.	The bitch has more confidence, so someone else's mood doesn't have much impact. Instead she plays tennis.
He is the boss . . . of her.	She stays the boss . . . of herself.
The nice girl treats her interests as "little things" or secondary.	The bitch doesn't treat her interests as minor little things. They are *her* things.
He is the boss . . . of her.	She stays the boss . . . of herself.
The nice girl gives too much first, and then negotiates reciprocity later.	The bitch gives *only* when it is reciprocal.
He is the boss . . . of her.	She stays the boss . . . of herself.

When a relationship starts off at lightning speed, the man will at some point pull back to regain his need for space and then the woman will be left off-balance. It's then that the nice girl appears needy, trying to "win back" his affections. This is when she jumps through hoops. A man loses respect for a woman who needs his approval, particularly when she will overcompensate to get it.

A man needs to "bring offerings." He needs to be on his toes a little bit. He has to make sure his shoes are tied, his pants are pulled up, and his manners are existent. When he opens car doors, when he minds his p's and q's, and when he shows his best manners, it means she has his respect. In this way, she remains a bit of a bitch in his eyes because he has to keep himself in check; he doesn't relax in terms of how he behaves around her.

ATTRACTION PRINCIPLE #46
The second a woman works overtime to make herself fit his criteria, she has lowered the standard of that relationship.

As long as a woman stays in control of remaining who she is, he will need her. When a man thinks about a woman who has control over herself, he automatically thinks about her preferences and about ways to please her.

Women are much more likely to cancel plans. Men don't give up "boys' night out." Men don't give up their work, or their sleep, or their food. (Most don't even give up their mothers.) Likewise, they respect a woman who will hold onto what is important to her.

When was the last time you heard a guy call his barber and say, "Yeah, Sam . . . I'll need to cancel my 2:15 haircut. Sally and I need to spend more time bonding." It just ain't happening. It doesn't matter if you swung from the chandelier the night before with show-stopping sex accompanied by screaming that scared off the alley cats. At 2:15, your man will belong to Sam. Men can shift gears from romantic to practical—and so can the bitch. She speaks to him in his own language.

The nice girl, however, is too needy to let go. "But he did all of the pursuing," says the nice girl. This may be true, but you have the power to decide when you show up—and this is how you stay the boss of you.

Even in a racing event, the car has to pull into the pit to have the tires changed or it won't be able to stay on the track, it won't be able to control its direction, and it will lose traction. Men don't always think long term, so if you let him control the speed, he's likely to let the relationship crash at high speed into a wall. As the adage goes, "The candle that burns twice as bright burns half as long." That's why you absolutely must set the pace and keep your own rhythm. Otherwise, he'll have you jumping through hoops. Again, it doesn't matter if he wants to see you constantly. Even if he's an incredible guy and you feel great temptation, *don't give him all of your time*.

In the beginning, try to see him two-thirds of the time that he asks. For the remaining third, you have "something else going on." Don't sit at home twiddling your thumbs waiting for his next call. Keep in mind that this isn't about "playing hard to get." *Keep it real*. Force yourself to keep the routine you had before you met him. Once you lose your rhythm, you lose your psychological equilibrium and you become needy.

My former roommate Gale was always very good at this. She'd often turn off her ringer and wouldn't take any calls. In the afternoon, if she felt tired and wanted to stay home for the evening, she'd cancel her date. She'd have a glass of wine and chill with a good book or her favorite TV program. Gale always had a quality man pursuing her.

Being a bitch isn't about exuding a certain kind of arrogance. Contrary to what the media would have us believe, it doesn't matter how "hip," "cool," or "cocky" you appear to be. Power is the control you have over yourself. In fact, when a woman is trying too hard to be "cocky," she's usually not moving to her own rhythm because she's trying too hard to convince herself that she is stronger than she really is.

As Gregory Corso said, "Standing on a street corner

waiting for no one is power." When you don't wait for anyone, it's because you don't *need* anyone. When you approach men this way, any man who steps up to the plate will have to meet you at your level. First, you have to stop needing his approval—only then will your needs be met.

For example, Lynn had just started dating a plastic surgeon named Kevin. They had separate residences, and one night she cooked dinner for him. He called at the last minute to cancel their preplanned dinner date because he had switched shifts with another surgeon. Lynn had already cooked an elaborate meal. His call came only a half-hour before he was supposed to show up. Had he called her early in the day right after he agreed to switch shifts, she wouldn't have labored tirelessly.

Here's where she made a mistake of jumping through hoops. She offered to cook the same dinner again the following night. *And* she agreed to drive to his place to do it. What she should have done is put "the skids" on the cooking plans altogether. She should have said, "*Mmm.* It's really good, Kevin. Too bad you missed out."

When a man treats a woman with disrespect and she takes it, he begins to lose respect for her. Predictably, Lynn was at Kevin's place the following evening; he wasn't appreciative, which hurt her feelings. They stopped dating a short while later.

A bitch prioritizes herself over "melting" into someone else. Because of this, her no means *no,* and her yes means *yes.* The objective isn't to be obnoxious but to have the ability to be clear. You can be very nice and still be clear. A man will respect a woman who is clear and direct about what she needs, without waffling or second-guessing herself. If a man is late for a date, for example, the bitch will become annoyed because she is inconvenienced. Annoyance is different than becoming emotional. She'll say something more along the lines of, "Don't waste my time. If you are going to be late, please let me know so I can make other arrangements. I have better things I can be doing with my time than waiting around."

If he chooses not to respect her the next time around, she allows fifteen or twenty minutes and then leaves without him. Her time and priorities are important to her. At no time does she give herself up.

When you're in this type of situation, ask yourself the following questions: What does this look like from his vantage point? What message am I sending by my reactions to his behavior?

Your true power, therefore, is marked by:

- Realizing what your rhythm is, and moving to it
- Knowing who you are, and what you will or will not accept
- Having the ability to make a decision *without* second-guessing yourself afterward, and without being talked out of how you feel
- Having self-control, because *true* power is the control you have over *yourself*

When you have control of yourself, you don't need to be emotional all the time. When you have a sassy "edge," you stay the boss . . . of you. Ironically, this is also when you become the boss . . . of him.

From Sappy to Sassy

Whenever a woman is too emotional or sappy, it can be too much for a man, especially with a woman he barely knows. The bitch is sassier, which is easier for a man to deal with. It's similar to the rougher tone men use to speak to one another.

One man described a perfect example of how men get spooked by too much sappy emotional talk, particularly early on in the relationship. He was put off by receiving several tear-jerking Hallmark cards from a woman he'd just met.

Another example of this is a man who was constantly read poems by a woman he'd just met. "They always seemed so long and drawn out. Some of them were short and boring. But the one thing in common is that they all sucked. 'My love for thee.' Or, 'My heart is heavy with love and it's pushing against my rib cage.' And she'd cry when she read them. I started avoiding her calls."

One man described dating a woman whom he'd known for three weeks. He said, "A man doesn't need to hear a woman tell him that she loves him every thirty seconds. This woman said it over and over again. It was like dating a cockatoo . . . Love you . . . Love you . . . Love you . . . Love you . . . Love you!"

Men also notice if you are trying too hard to get into a relationship. Do you have twelve sappy relationship books about feelings on your coffee table? Do you have an ad running in the "personals" while you pursue online dating? Do you have that one pushy girlfriend who gives you away? You walk into your home with him after a date and you hit the play button on your answering machine. "Hey, girlfriend. There's another singles event at the car wash this Sunday. Free coffee. And I hear there's a new batch of divorcés coming through. The early bird catches the worm!"

Being sassy means you won't knock yourself out. The minute a man feels you're trying too hard, the challenge is over. Once you accidentally step into that arena, you have to win him back by showing him that you won't wait. You have a life. You have other priorities, some of which come before him.

ATTRACTION PRINCIPLE #47
You jump through hoops any time you repeatedly make it very obvious you're giving your "all."

- Don't talk for hours on the phone before your first date. Joke around. Be sassy. Make your plans or arrangements to meet and then politely end the conversation.
- Don't discuss deep issues in the beginning. Don't use catch phrases from therapy like *cathartic, processing, triggered, owning it,* or *inner child.* Don't make chicken soup and tell him you "wanna midwife each other's soul."
- If you believe in astrology, don't tell him that you can only get together when Mercury is "tiptoeing" around the moon, making a three-week "retrograde" around Jupiter (with a quick stop for coffee on Pluto).
- Don't tell him who you were in a "past life," or what you plan to come back as in your next one. He'll think your cheese is sliding off the cracker.

- In the beginning, avoid seeing him more than one night in a row. Start out seeing him one to two nights a week.

- Don't pout or whimper when he doesn't call. You have to make him wonder every now and then about what you're doing when you're not with him. When you regulate the timing, it keeps him wanting and it charges up his batteries.

- If he takes you to a nice restaurant, don't order a celery stick "with oil and vinegar on the side," and then continue to nibble off his plate like a hummingbird. Don't be so nervous or concerned with impressing him with your table etiquette. Have an appetite for enjoying life.

- Don't disclose over your first dinner what you're "working through" from childhood.

- Don't try to fix his flaws either. I know one woman who bought a man the book *Tuesdays with Morrie*. She thought the book would help him with his workaholism. Too much psychological analysis comes across as too sappy.

- Don't accompany him when he goes out with his friends. You don't want to be one of the "boys."

- Don't do any slow drive-bys with your headlights turned off to see if he's at home. And no high-speed flybys, either.

- If he calls you and asks you to come over late at night after he's been out with his friends, don't happily go skipping over, kicking your heels together like Julie Andrews in *The Sound of Music*.

- Don't date someone who has addictions of any kind,

hoping to "help" him by going to AA meetings with him. Let him work out his own stuff. If he can't treat himself well, he'll never treat you well.

- Never call more than once in a row, even if his machine cuts you short. Don't leave long mushy messages. Keep the messages friendly, but short and sweet.

- Don't e-mail more than once in a row or send long e-mails about "feelings," "issues," and what you "need" that you aren't getting. If he sends you an e-mail, don't respond within thirty seconds each and every time.

- Don't stop eating, sleeping, or exercising. Keep your routine. If he wants to spend more time with you than you can comfortably give, invite him to join you in one of your activities—like a walk with your dog or going for a weekend bike ride.

- Avoid last-minute dates because you "miss him."

- Don't walk in the door, check your messages, and call him right back. Settle in, take a bath or shower, eat dinner, and relax. Move to your own rhythm, and then call back. He has to know you have a life . . . *every* day.

- If you're on the phone and you get another call that beeps through, don't say "Stay right there. Don't hang up! Whoever it is, I'll get rid of him!" When you do come back on the line, don't always be so quick to report the identity of the other caller. "That was the vet. Tigger had an earache."

- Don't regularly travel forty minutes in traffic to see him because you have a roommate and he has his own place. Look at a map and take note: It's just as far from his house to your house as it is from your house to his house. So don't feel guilty about having him come your way.

- Don't ask for affection. Don't coax affection out of him. Don't give affection when he isn't being affectionate. If he's ignoring you, don't try harder. "Honey, can I give you a backrub?"

- Don't be a slave to the phone. Don't play his voice message back to your girlfriend to dissect every detail of your situation. Pay attention to the big picture. Does he add to your life as a whole, and do you feel good after he's been around? (If not, "fast forward" the message and hit "delete.")

- Don't memorize his phone number in the first week of dating or call him all the time and hang up. He'll know it's you.

- If he's in a bad mood, make an excuse and then go do your own thing.

- Above all, make every concerted effort to stay focused on *your* life. That's how you stay sassy in his eyes.

ATTRACTION PRINCIPLE #48
You have to keep from being sucked down into quicksand. Unless you maintain control over yourself, the relationship is doomed.

Basic Bitch 101

A man notices something from the very first phone message that he leaves on a woman's answering service: whether she is trying too hard. She may be trying too hard to impress him; she may be trying too hard to win him over; or she may be trying too hard to be sexy. Whether she is too needy or trying too hard, it has the same effect. *The bitch never tries that hard to make an impression.*

He dials her number and the machine picks up. *Beep!* Then comes the breathy voice, which sounds as if she's half asleep. "Hello there. You've reached Susan's answering service. I am out and about and just a little bit busy at the moment doing, well, [giggle] . . . If you would be sooooooo kind to leave a message after the tone, I will try my very best to get back to you as soooooooon as I am available. Although I just got in from Portugal, I haven't quite unpacked yet. But if I have a free moment, I'll call you. Wait for the beep . . . *ciao* . . . ta, ta . . . kisses . . . have a spiritual day . . . and bless you for calling me." *Beep!* All she needs is a 900 number and a pimp, and girlfriend is in business.

As men often say, "Men like a woman who is natural." This has nothing to do with makeup or dyed hair. Natural does not mean he wants a vegetarian who drinks wheat-grass juice or a woman who wears organic lip-gloss. Natural implies that the minute something is excessive it becomes a turn-off, because it looks as if a woman is *trying too hard to get the attention.* Whenever a woman is trying too hard, she is jumping through hoops.

ATTRACTION PRINCIPLE #49

**Jumping through hoops often has a negative outcome:
He sees it as an opportunity to have his cake and eat it,
too. But when you stay just outside his reach, he'll stay
on his best behavior.**

Let's look at how one relationship unfolded when the woman was willing to jump through hoops. It's a classic scenario. Sarah bought an airplane ticket to go see Mickey, a man she'd met only once before when he had been in town for a holiday weekend. They'd kept in touch for a month via e-mail and over the phone. Convinced he was "the one," Sarah decided she'd like to see Mickey again.

The ticket cost $400. Mickey agreed to pay for the accommodations, which ended up being $40 for a motel. After Sarah arrived, they had sex in the motel. Then he took her to a coffee shop with coupons that were complimentary with the room. Afterward they had sex again—*while* he watched the World Series.

A Kodak moment, isn't it? No foreplay. No candle. No soft music. No showering together. Instead, one eye is on the game, and he's listening for the score. "The count is three to two . . . and the bases are loaded. *Steeeeerike!*" Any man—even one who was raised in a jail—has sense enough to know that watching a game while having sex is rude. Hardly a "romantic getaway" for two. After two days of being romantic, they couldn't wait to "getaway" from each other.

Now let's do a financial comparison. He got plenty of food, plenty of sex, and he got to watch the game (not bad for $40). Her bill exceeded $400. She did, however, get two extra packets of peanuts on the airplane, each containing 2.5 peanuts, for a total of five peanuts. Even if she divided them up into peanut halves, she still wouldn't come out ahead.

A bitch would never have put herself in this position. She would have required that he come to see her, *and* she would have suggested a hotel that is conveniently located.

When the nice girl jumps through hoops or bends over backward and overcompensates, she does so because she has a fantasy that he will "complete her." To keep the spark from fizzling, it's sometimes best to stay ever-so-slightly just outside a man's reach, because it charges up his batteries.

The nice girl fails to take a "breather" because of her fantasy that he is "the one" or her "soul mate." But this fantasy is a liability because it feeds a myopic view that he is the center of her life.

Another reason women rush into a relationship is *fear*. A woman named Mary said, "I can't say 'no' to my boyfriend. For example, I drive to his place and I wait outside in my car until he comes home from work. Then I eat dinner later and I stay up late even though I have to be up early. I feel totally depleted the next day."

I asked Mary why she doesn't just say, "Not tonight, honey. I really need some down time." She answered, "Because then he pouts. I guess deep down I'm afraid he'll get another girlfriend."

The bitch is not governed by fear of losing a man, because she knows the real price to pay is when she loses *herself*. Almost immediately, women give themselves up *in small ways*. The cumulative effect of these subtle concessions, however, is what amounts to feeling depleted.

Here's the cycle:

- She develops a myopic view that what he gives is absolutely vital.
- Because of this fantasy, she gives up everyday needs.
- She feels more and more drained but continues to try harder, believing that he'll be the one to make her feel fulfilled again.
- He senses her willingness to exert herself, and *relaxes* what he gives even more.
- She senses this and works even harder to jump through hoops.
- The cycle gets worse, as she becomes more and more depleted.

The solution? Lose the fantasy. And if you feel you are going to resent something after you give it, don't give it. Give only what feels comfortable to give. This will enable you to stay firmly planted with both feet on the ground.

Remember when you learned the golden rule in kindergarten? This was a nice theory, but in the real world we'll need to modify it just a bit.

LET'S REPLACE . . .	WITH . . .
"Do unto others as you would have others do unto you."	"Do unto others, after they show you they are worthy."
"Love conquers all."	"Love conquers her, when she gives all."
"To give is better than to receive."	"It is better to give *and* receive."

(*continued*)

LET'S REPLACE . . .	WITH . . .
"Charity begins at home."	"There is no charity case in this home."
"All's well that ends well."	"All's well for those who cover their 'ends' well."
"Love thy neighbor."	"Love thyself first, and your neighbor will be happier living next to you."

ATTRACTION PRINCIPLE #50
The nice girl gives away too much of herself when pleasing him regularly becomes more important than pleasing herself.

Many times, when you are going through your daily life, Attraction Principle #50 will be very subtle. For example, a woman may have spread herself very thin between her career and her time to herself, and she's exhausted. He asks her out: "How about Wednesday?" She tells him Wednesday isn't good because of work demands on Thursday morning. So he asks, "How about Tuesday or Thursday?" Then she accepts. Her needs are swept under the rug, and worse yet, *she* is doing the sweeping. Then she goes out and she is cranky and irritated because she is overworked and hasn't rested.

The bitch doesn't take the more difficult course; she takes the easier course. How hard is it to suggest, "The weekend would really be better." It's better for *everyone* involved. The bitch is her own guide.

Cathy was on a first date when she found that the guy wouldn't let her order what she wanted off the menu. He kept saying, "You *have* to try this . . ." She was firm but polite, and finally, he ordered what she wanted. Then he ordered a bottle of wine after she had said she didn't want to "drink and drive," particularly because it was a weeknight. He poured her a glass and they made a toast, so she didn't argue. They clinked glasses and she took one sip to be gracious, but not another sip thereafter. Her glass of wine didn't move.

What is important in this example is that she didn't explain herself. She just did what she wanted to do. She didn't need to ask his permission to honor her own wishes, she just honored them.

Another woman I know shared a story about a man she dated. After two dates, the man asked her to take him to the airport at 4 A.M. (yes, in the morning).

On their second date, he was coordinating while she listened. "You could get up at 4 A.M., pick me up at 5 A.M., get to the airport at 6 A.M., go home by 7 A.M., shower, and get to work by 8 A.M." (The ringmaster had the poodle hoop-circuit all planned out.) Here's a novel idea that never crossed his mind: He could pay seven bucks for a shuttle, rather than yank her out of bed at such a ridiculous hour. She politely said, "I'm sorry. I'm going to be busy." And he said, "What do you mean busy? Busy what? Sleeping?" She smiled and politely said, "Yes."

If he acts as though it's perfectly normal for you to jump through hoops, don't let that be your guide. Ignore what he says. When he says, "I'm spiritual," don't listen. Just look at how he acts. If he said he was spiritual, but he expects a lot of "unholy compromising," let your observations be your guide.

Another way a woman may jump through hoops is to "tell time" by when a man calls. How many times have you called a girlfriend to say let's "hook up" and she has to wait for a call from a guy she's dating to give you an answer? These are always the women who get treated poorly. She becomes depleted because she is willing to wait "at bay," never making plans until she rules out the possibility "beyond a reasonable doubt" that she is seeing a man. Then you get a call back, "Okay let's get together," but now it's 10 P.M.

If you don't hear from him in enough time to suggest he respects your time, there is a simple solution: Don't give him any.

Here's an example of a woman who jumps through hoops—and at the same time, it defies the stereotype that beauty and youth are what are most attractive to a man. Karla was nineteen and so pretty you could have placed her on the cover of any men's magazine without airbrushing. She was the one who cried on my shoulder about the fact that her boyfriend, Bart, told her that when he goes out with his friends he looks at the sixteen-year-olds.

Now let's hear Bart's version: "I'm not in love with her the way she is with me." He shared with me a story of when she was doing his laundry for him in his apartment. "I was being a total jerk. You know what she said to me? 'After I finish your laundry, I'm going home.' There were three more loads, and she did them. I really would have respected her if she had said, 'Screw you' and walked out."

A tip: When you are at his place any day of the week, don't do any housework. The only laundry you do is your own. The only tub you scrub is your own. The only person you clean up after is yourself. If his place is a mess, go to yours. If he asks you to help him clean, be subtle. Just tell him the maidservant has the day off on Sundays.

ATTRACTION PRINCIPLE #51
The relationship may not be right for you if you find yourself jumping through hoops. When something is right, it will feel easier and much more effortless.

Just remember, it isn't about a man. This is your life . . . and it's too precious to waste. Do things when it is convenient, especially if it regards your relationships of choice and who you let in on the "inside." It will yield a much better return on investment . . . especially in the dignity department.

6

NAGGING

No

MORE

What to Do When He Takes You for Granted and Nagging Doesn't Work

" Well done is better than well said. "

—BEN FRANKLIN

A Lover or a Mother?

It's a scenario that is all too familiar: a nice girl on "over-drive" trying to please her man. He comes home from work and she tries to have a conversation. He tunes her out saying, "I'm tired." She makes dinner, but he eats in front of the TV so he can watch *Monday Night Football*. She tries to look pretty; he doesn't notice. But watch what happens when he realizes the swimsuit issue got delivered; he almost hyper-ventilates. Diagnosis? She feels taken for granted.

Like the bum on the street with a sign that says *Will work for food*, your sign now reads *Will work for attention*. Well, no more "slummin,'" girlfriend. We are under new manage-ment. Under the old management, you dealt with his lack of attention by nagging. And if you'll notice, it hasn't worked. This is why all of the steps discussed in this chapter involve changes in demeanor. When you nag at a man, he becomes more reclusive.

Essentially, you always want to remember that although he is a grown man, inside there is a three-year-old causing him to have Appreciation Deficit Disorder. Whenever you nag, you activate this toddler, and you have a thirty second window before you've activated the "little boy gland."

It's as easy as changing a radio station. In thirty seconds, he'll tune you out and won't tune you back in until the nag-ging is over. It doesn't matter if his pants are on fire and smoke has filled the room. He won't hear a word you say. This is why you should communicate with your actions . . . rather than your words. Since a man won't discuss feelings as a woman does, anything past the second repetition seems like nagging. Never ask a man to do something more than twice or he'll feel as though he's being scolded by Mom. And whenever you nag, he'll behave like a stubborn teenager and rebel.

ATTRACTION PRINCIPLE #52
When you nag, he tunes you out. But when you speak with your actions, he pays attention.

Women often say, "Little boys are so sweet. What changes?" According to Freud, it gets messed up somewhere around the potty-training years. To better understand the origin of the "little boy gland" and to see how a man takes a woman for granted, let's now turn our attention to examine the behavior of a toddler.

A three-year-old wants to be independent of Mommy, but he also wants to take for granted that she is still right there within his reach. So he tests to see how far he can go. The disobedient little boy wobbles around a corner mischievously and pauses. Then he runs back around the corner to make sure Mommy's still right there.

With a grown man, there's one extra step in the middle. After he wobbles off but before he runs back, he will turn to look over his shoulder to see, "What will Mommy do next? Does she nag? Does she panic? Will she chase me?" Your reaction determines whether he'll take one step closer or another step farther away.

ATTRACTION PRINCIPLE #53
**When a man takes a woman for granted,
he still looks for reassurance
that she is still "right there."**

Think about how futile nagging is. It gives him the reassurance that he can continue to be distant and you will still be there. Very little is negotiated with words. He doesn't sit down and say, "Look, I want to be lazy in this relationship. But I'd like you to keep cooking me meals and I'd like you to keep having sex with me whenever it is convenient for me. In fact, I'm a little horny right now . . . wanna hop on?"

One would think a woman who'd accept these terms would have to be high on crack. Yet women accept these terms every day. Nonstop. "What went wrong?" she asks. In the beginning he went out of his way to show her he's a gentleman; he opened car doors, he let her order first, and so on. So he knows how to treat a woman. The slacking off happens gradually without any negotiation and certainly without her consent, so she doesn't fully realize it is happening until things have gotten so off course. Then she nags to try to get them back on.

Once a woman realizes a man is going into "couch potato" mode, she often mistakenly tries to address it. "You never take me out or bring me flowers anymore." Or, "We never spend time together." This is a sign to a man that he *has her right where he wants her.* Now he doesn't participate because, in his mind, all it takes to satisfy her is his presence. He quips, "I'm with you, aren't I?"

To get the three-year-old to run back to Mommy, she has to stay just *outside his reach.* The reason nagging keeps her within his reach is that he senses she is "locked down" waiting for him. She may be waiting for him to give more, participate more, or be more attentive in some way. But she's still waiting. *On hold.*

The only thing worse than him being locked in a cage is the feeling that he has you locked in his. Hence the need for a 180-degree change as prescribed in this chapter.

When he takes you for granted, you've triggered the same kind of love he had for his mother, grandmother, or some other woman who raised him. Now you've become "old faithful." No matter how much you scream at him, he knows you aren't going anywhere. "She may kick my ass, but she'll still love me and I can do whatever I want." And it's this very security blanket you *don't* want him to have.

Men know it's wrong, but they'll still try to see how far they can push the envelope. As one man said to me, "Men will get away with what you let them get away with." That isn't to say there aren't great guys out there. But a man with integrity, or anyone with integrity for that matter, doesn't want something they haven't earned. That's why a high-caliber self-respecting guy will be attracted to a woman who won't let someone walk all over her.

If he takes you for granted and you pull back a little with no explanation, it catches him off-guard and gets his attention bigtime. You're no longer acting in a way he is used to and you are no longer his mommy. This action generates desire for you as a lover. But if you posture yourself as "old faithful," he'll perceive you as his mother and he'll take you for granted.

Failure to get enough attention isn't the only thing women complain about. Often women nag about household chores. Again, you have to condition him *without* words. Most men don't particularly care if the place doesn't look great or if it's messy. Most guys are happy to come home and plunk down on the couch with the worn-out spot and his butt imprint on it. He doesn't care if the sink is full of dishes from the day before or that his shoes left muddy prints all over the carpet.

ATTRACTION PRINCIPLE #54
**When the routine becomes predictable,
he's more likely to give you the same type of
love he had for his mother—and the odds
that he will take you for granted increase.**

When you're standing in a grocery line and you look at people with children, you'll notice that the mother who has control over her child doesn't nag or holler. She says one sentence or she gives the child a look. Because the child respects her and he is not sure what will happen next, he'll straighten up. Words are not needed to teach a man how to treat you. A little bit of silence or distance will often do the trick.

Sometimes as a lover you will have to set forth terms that

are also in the best interest of the "diapered one." Why? *He is a man.* And there will forever be a three-year-old trapped inside him.

All of the behavioral changes discussed in this chapter allow you to keep a calm, charming, and pleasant demeanor. The objective is to avoid being his mother and to make the transition back to being his lover.

A man can't correlate sexual feelings with feelings for his mother. So be careful of the female figure that you become in his life. To stay his lover, you have to keep him on his toes. This behavior incites his interest and makes him come your way. He is happier being your lover than he is when you become his mother. Granted, he looks comfortable and content on the couch. But he isn't content when you become his mother because he no longer has a lover . . . and neither do you.

The balance of this chapter gives you insight into how to turn things around and bring him back to pursuit mode when his mind drifts elsewhere. Men are hunters. What he gets from the nice girl is a protective kind of motherly love that lessens his sexual desire. He doesn't pursue his mom. What the nice girl needs to understand is that it takes the heat out of it for a man when you give him a predictable security blanket.

Women often reassure, or try to convince, a man to win him over. But the bitch wins him over by acting as though she could take him or leave him. Therefore, backing off in a subtle way will give your man renewed "pep" in his step. You can also apply the advice in this chapter:

- When he seems complacent
- When he waffles about whether to be in the relationship

- When he isn't respectful
- When he repeatedly ignores what you need

Let's get started. Do not pass Go, do not collect $200—because sister, there will be plenty of time for that later.

R_x: *Treat Him Like a Friend*

Think back to the beginning of your relationship when you first met your partner. You didn't nag him. Chances are, you treated him much as you would a friend. You were relaxed; you had fun and laughed more. You felt comfortable speaking your mind. He wasn't the "be all and end all" of your existence.

When you started nagging, your behavior began to tell a different story. "I'm affected by every move you make." For this reason and this reason alone, nagging rewards him. Not because he enjoys it, but because it reassures him you care.

ATTRACTION PRINCIPLE #55
**Negative attention is still attention.
It lets a man know that he has you—
right where he wants you.**

It doesn't matter if you're a high-powered litigation attorney and can give a closing argument that makes his head spin. Nagging still reassures him of where he stands and where you stand. It doesn't give him anything to worry about, think about, or mull over. It doesn't intrigue him or pull him in. Instead, he tunes you out.

Now you want to "talk" and he wants to do anything *except* talk. And if you press the issue, he'll shift the blame.

How to Shift the Blame . . .
The Textbook Guide

- First, tell her that the timing to discuss it isn't right. Remember, it's never a good time to "talk."

- Before hearing a word, tell her she took everything wrong and is being "too sensitive."

- Get a rotation going: Monday and Wednesday she's "overreacting." Tuesday and Thursday she's "blowing it out of proportion." And on weekends she's "imagining things."

- Change the subject. Say, "You're starting your period, aren't you?"

- If this doesn't work, pick a fight. Be very combative, but repeatedly point out that **she** was the one who started the argument.

- If she has six good points, and you have one semi-good little point, place all of the emphasis on your *one semi-good little point*.

- Don't veer. Keep asking about your one little point over and over, then demand a quick answer. If she hesitates, use this as evidence that you are right.

(continued)

How to Shift the Blame . . .
The Textbook Guide

- If she is clearly right, find fault with her that has nothing to do with the incident, and use that.

- Be sure to create your own imaginary panel of experts (composed of people she's never met). Say, "Even Joe and Jim agree with me and think you are being completely unreasonable."

- When she tries to explain the same thing in a different way, roll your eyes.

- Appoint yourself her in-house therapist. Say, "You do this to **yourself**. **Why** do you do this to yourself?"

- Keep count of how many times she repeats herself, and be sure to remind her.

- It's like boxing. Jab with the left; uppercut with the right. Then run . . .

- As Muhammad Ali used to say: "Float like a butterfly; sting like a bee." Float by dodging the issue, and sting by asking why she "can't let it go."

- Keep dancing, and stay **light** on those feet.

- And, remember, it's always **her** fault. That's your story, and you are **stickin'** to it.

The other thing he'll do is tune you out completely. He can see lips moving, but he cannot hear what you are saying. Like a remote control in his head, you've been "muted." Ideally, his hope is that you'll "nag yourself silly" to the point of exhaustion. He figures if he bides his time, eventually you'll wear yourself out and go away.

Women differ in terms of how long it takes them to run out of steam. Evidently, according to the men I interviewed, each woman—as with clothing, perfume, and lovemaking—has her own "personalized style" of nagging. Here are some just to name a few:

- **The Marathon Nagger:** This woman will nag for a longer time so she paces herself, for two to three hours.
- **The Sprint Nagger:** This woman will nag for a shorter period of time. It's a more intense burst, so she'll get tired much more quickly.
- **The Momentum Whiner:** This woman will start out with a whine and then will slowly pick up momentum, building up to a nag. Then she'll cry. The longer she goes, the more momentum she builds and the less likely she is to stop.
- **The Sunrise Whiner:** It starts as the sun comes up over the horizon. His eyes begin to open and he hears his first morning whine. Or he's still asleep, and it wakes him like a rooster.
- **The Nightcap Nagger:** Just as he is falling into a deep REM sleep, she nudges him and reminds him of something he has to do the following day.
- **The Bushwhacker:** This nagger employs the element of surprise. She catches him off-guard at any moment in the day. One minute everything is going along fine and then, without any warning, she jumps out of the bushes and whacks him.
- **The Sniper:** This is the premeditated nagger who will make one cutting remark. It's usually a well-placed shot that delivers a devastating blow.

Many times, when a man steps on a woman's toes, he doesn't have a clue. She has to remember that if something happens that she doesn't like, he may not know any better.

Therefore, if she wants to tell him something he did that put her off, she should stay calm. Then she should say, "Could I explain something to you?" She needs to approach it as though he did not intend to hurt her because more often than not he *doesn't have an inkling.*

Shaquille O'Neal said, "This is a tough game. There are times when you've got to play hurt, when you've got to block out the pain." The reason that you block out the pain is that it impairs your decision-making. Long term, how you communicate will affect his desire for you.

If a woman is losing a man's attention, it's because the woman is following a *predictable* routine and she's becoming an opponent rather than a partner. Therefore:

Nagging = A woman who is predictable = A feeling of obligation = Decreased lust

Indifference = Less predictable response = Renewed interest

ATTRACTION PRINCIPLE #56
When you treat him casually as though he's a friend, he'll come your way. Because he wants things to be romantic, but he also *wants* to be the pursuer.

Envisioning him as just a friend enables you to relate to him without the heaviness or the intensity of the nagging. Don't say, "Hey, buddy. Hey pal," and throw down a cold beer in front of him with a fake, peppermint-refreshing smile. Don't offer to girl-watch with him or chew tobacco. Don't overdo it.

Again, treat him as you would a friend, which means exude a demeanor that seems *unlikely given the circumstances.* If you've been uptight, needy, or clingy, appearing casual, relaxed, and *un*concerned is the unlikely response that he would expect.

For example, if he has excuses for why he isn't spending time with you, you need to make excuses for why you can't spend time with *him*. Is it a game? No. If he's too busy and you've already tried telling him how you feel, it's time to show him with your actions that he will no longer be dictating the terms. Because his terms will most likely continue to drive a wedge between you—and that's not the outcome you want.

ATTRACTION PRINCIPLE #57
A little distance combined with the appearance of self-control makes him nervous that he may be losing you.

Here is a classic case in point. You want to see more of him and you suggest going away for the weekend together. He says, "No, I can't because of work." You've typically whined over the issue of him not spending enough time with you. What will throw him and get his attention is if you go left when he thinks you'll go right.

If you *don't* cop an attitude or you appear to lose interest in going away, he'll immediately be concerned. Most men are used to women wanting to be around them all the time. He gets concerned when he's busy trying to defend something you mysteriously no longer want. If you don't bring it up and pretend to forget all about it, he second-guesses himself: "*Hmm* . . . why is this okay with her when I know it's wrong?" Now his clout or leverage with you will be called into question, and he no longer knows if he has a 100 percent hold on you. When he *doesn't* get the nagging but he *knows* he deserves it, he begins to wonder what's going on.

Let's say he likes seeing you two nights a week, but he likes to do his own thing on the weekends. Some weekends you get together and other weekends he leaves you hanging when he goes out with the boys. The last thing you want to let Yogi Bear think is that you are Boo Boo the fool. "Gee, Yogi what are we going to do next? Okay!"

You need to alter the pattern that has become convenient for him *with no attitude and no warning*. Use the same type of excuses that he wanted you to accept. See him half as much as he wants to see you. "I'd love to see you Thursday, but I can't. I am really behind in my work. I want to go to the gym after work, and I'm going to be too tired. We'll get together next week." In that one gesture, you've done something you could have never accomplished with all the whining and nagging in the world. You've just rekindled the flame.

The second you take away the security of a predictable routine, his orientation changes. Instead of worrying about buying time or making excuses about work, he has to think of something fun to do so you'll want to be with him. When you're not available, *he'll go out of his way to make more time for you.*

If you ask any parrot trainer how to train a parrot, he or she will tell you to raise the perch to about shoulder level. The trainer will tell you not to raise the bird up higher than you, because the bird will think he is better than you. No matter how much the bird loves you, if you put your finger up over your head to touch him, he'll be more inclined to bite you. This dynamic with birds is where the term *cocky* originated.

If, on the other hand, you put the bird on the ground, the bird feels vulnerable. Trainers suggest doing this to keep the bird "in check." If you put your finger out, instead of biting you, he'll crawl up on your finger and want to get on your arm. When your man behaves as though he is more worthy than you, re-create the balance and equality in the relationship by gently taking the "little birdie" and putting him on the ground.

ATTRACTION PRINCIPLE #58
A man takes a woman for granted when he's interested, but will no longer go out of his way.

For example, Rhonda was being taken for granted by her boyfriend. He asked her to "come over" late one night. She indicated she didn't have a car because it was in the shop. He was seven minutes away with a car that was running fine, parked right there in his driveway. He asked, "So, Rhonda, when will your car be ready?" After realizing that she had no wheels, he dropped the subject of getting together.

In this example, Rhonda was "dissed" by a guy who wanted

her to keep him warm at night but wouldn't drive seven minutes to pick her up. Typically, she would have nagged, but she didn't this time. The next time he called, Rhonda spoke to him very casually as though he were an acquaintance. A friend. A pal. A *muchacho*. She said, "Hey, great to hear from you. Can you call me back in a few? I am on the other line." He called back and she was in the shower. Then he called a third time. They chatted a bit casually. For the first time in their relationship, her disposition changed from *intense* to *indifferent*. After a short while, her call waiting beeped through and she politely ended the conversation. "Talk to you soon. Bye, sweetie." Almost immediately, the guy started to become much more attentive.

Let's hit the "pause" button. Rewind . . . now, let's review play-by-play. Notice how simple it was for Rhonda to get him to realize he needs to give more.

1. He wasn't nice.
2. He *knows* he wasn't nice.
3. He expected her to nag.
4. She didn't nag.
5. He was unsure.
6. She was relaxed and self-assured.
7. She gave no explanation and no attitude.
8. He said to himself, "Uh oh. I better get busy."

ATTRACTION PRINCIPLE #59
**When you nag, *you* become the problem,
and he deals with it by tuning you out.
But when you don't nag, he deals with *the problem*.**

When there is a problem, men love to "fix" it. By nagging, you make it seem as though the problem lies with you. A perfect example is Diana, who started nagging her husband to fix a latch in the laundry room. After the third time she asked, he became so irritated that no force on earth could get him to fix that latch.

One evening some friends came over. While her husband was within earshot, Diana asked her friend's husband to fix the latch in the laundry room, in that sweet "damsel in distress" tone of voice that men eat up. Then she started looking for a screwdriver. Before she could even turn around, her husband ran up the stairs like Speedy Gonzales and fixed the latch in two minutes flat.

Men despise it when other men fix things for them. It's a territorial thing—like some other man is treading on his turf. When you've asked him to do something a few times and he doesn't do it, say, "Honey, it's okay. I don't need you to do it anymore. Ed, our next-door neighbor, said he'd come over and do it." If you don't have a neighbor, tell him his best friend will come do it. This is how you will get whatever it is you want done, right then and there.

My friend Lucy noticed that when she asked her husband for help in various ways, he was less attentive. For example, she often asked him to help bring in the groceries when she came back from the market. He was always in the middle of something, so he said, "Give me a minute." A minute later she said, "The food is going to spoil." And she kept repeating herself. "The food is going to go bad. If you're going to do it, please do it now." Every time she went to the market, it became a power struggle.

Then she stopped asking for his help and she noticed

a change. When she brought in the groceries and he asked if she wanted a hand she said, "No thanks, sweetie. I've got it." Suddenly, he was out there insisting on bringing in the groceries.

Then there's my friend Rayanna, who found herself repeatedly nagging her husband to take their child to school. He always made excuses to avoid doing the driving. But instead of nagging him, Rayanna found a single dad down the street to carpool with. When her husband got wind of the fact that a neighbor was doing the driving, suddenly Papa Bear put a chauffeur hat on.

ATTRACTION PRINCIPLE #60
If you take his chores away from him and praise someone else for doing it, he'll want his chores back.

Remember, men need a little coaxing. They aren't the most talented when it comes to running a household. Before he was Papa Bear, he lived the life of the untamed bear, living in his bachelor's habitat (with furniture). Think back to your first walk-through. The sheets didn't match and the pillows didn't have cases on them. His lamp consisted of a velour hand-me-down shade on a contemporary silver stand with air fresheners stuck to each side. It was so ugly that even the Salvation Army truck kept driving when you put it on the edge of the driveway.

So the day the "live-in bear" sets the living standard is the day your living standard plummets. Stake your claim, but do it without nagging him. There's a better way.

When you use guilt or nagging to motivate him, he feels bad. If you stroke his ego, however, he feels good. He needs to be praised. When he goes out to straighten the mailbox and he comes back inside, say, "Thank you so much, sweetie!" Praise him the whole way. Then he'll say, "Why don't I fix that latch in the laundry room?"

ATTRACTION PRINCIPLE #61
When you nag, he sees weakness.

Barbara told a funny story of how she engaged her husband in helping out one lazy Sunday afternoon. She sneaked down into the garage when her husband wasn't looking and figured out which circuit breaker turned off the lights to the part of the house he was in. Then she flipped it off and tiptoed back into the house and pretended as though she had no idea what happened. "Honey? I'm scared! What happened to the power?" He'd never think she had the brains to turn off a circuit breaker. Now she gave him a jolt with a jumper cable that got him right up off the couch. Big Papa to the rescue! Then he helped out because he felt needed—as the "man of the house."

He found a flashlight and went downstairs to the circuit-breaker box. He assigned her the very complicated duty of holding the flashlight for him. "Hold it steady." When he flipped the circuit breaker back on, she appeared proud and impressed. "Wow! I can't believe it. How did you do that?"

Then she called his mom. "Mom, he is so smart . . ."

When you make him feel like the man? The stud-muffin? The legend? You can ask him to do anything and he'll jump to do it. He won't do it because you nagged him, he'll do it because he *wants* to. And he'll now feel good about it.

As John Churton Collins said, "Never claim as a right what you can ask as a favor." Nagging makes it a right; asking for a favor makes it a positive experience. He'll come running to help if he's going to be praised. Just as a woman wants to be perceived as a "dream girl" to a man, a man wants to be perceived as a "hero" in his woman's eyes.

"Show" Is Better Than "Tell"

If you've been nagging and you want to get his attention, try something new on for size. Don't show your feelings for a little while. And don't explain why. Don't tell him that you've had an epiphany. Don't say this is the "new me." Don't exaggerate the change. "Feelings? What feelings?" Show—rather than tell—him that you aren't spilling your guts anymore.

Pop psychologists would suggest that you shouldn't withhold how you feel. They tell you to "express your-self." Begin every sentence with "I feel . . ." Ask for feed-back. Then sit in a circle, hold hands, and pass around the Kleenex. Promise never to do it again and live happily ever after. Then pay the therapist $175. It's a wonderful theoretical ideal. It feels warm and fuzzy just thinking about "expressing those feelings." And I'm sure on rare occasions it even works (because after spending $20,000 total on a therapist, you can't bear to think that it hasn't). But don't kid yourself. No man changes because of couples therapy. Men think of therapy as a form of blackmail—coercion with a ransom. The only reason they straighten up is to keep from going broke. Half a session will usually do the trick. "Okay. I'm all better. Can we stop the clock now?"

Expressing yourself when he takes you for granted doesn't work. You have to show him with actions. Expressing your feelings constantly is like pleading. It comes across as needy rather than dignified. But backing away when he crosses the line? *Plenty dignified.*

When he is intrigued because the cards aren't out on the table, he is forced to see you differently. It isn't the love he had for his mother. Or his sister. Or his grandma. Now you have his attention because he is no longer in the "safety zone" that enables him to have his cake and eat it, too.

This isn't being mean. Men are turned on by it. Think about the average run-of-the-mill male fantasy he had growing up: It's always a woman who has power over him. There's the teacher he had in the eighth grade, the nurse at the doctor's office, the babysitter who gave him a few extra cookies, the policewoman with the handcuffs. All of these women, in their own feminine ways, have power over him and leave him at a disadvantage and *he likes it.*

When you tell a man how you feel, most of the time he doesn't understand what you're talking about. You'll probably just confuse and frustrate him. If you take a look at Attraction Principle #62, you'll see what he *does* understand.

ATTRACTION PRINCIPLE #62
He perceives an emotional woman as more of a pushover.

My friend Gary races cars, and he shared a story about a girlfriend who nagged him. After a particular racing event, Gary was sitting next to his girlfriend in the stands. A couple of friendly women approached them and asked for his autograph. He recalls, "I couldn't believe my girlfriend got so upset because I didn't introduce her as my girlfriend. I just forgot, but she kept nagging. She even pouted." What he said next is interesting: "Do you know what the biggest turnoff is? A *martyr*."

We don't know if she overreacted because he may have been flirting up a storm. But what's interesting about this story is his choice of the word *martyr*. She was trying to use guilt to control and manipulate him; and men resent being manipulated. On the other hand, if she had backed off subtly, he'd have seen a woman who has pride and dignity—both of which are powerfully attractive qualities.

ATTRACTION PRINCIPLE #63
In the same way that familiarity breeds contempt, a slightly aloof demeanor can often renew his respect.

If a man isn't being nice when you're out, all you have to do is remain polite and then go home early. "I have a big day tomorrow. *[Yawn.]* We need to call this an early night." The next time you go out, he'll be on his best behavior.

An acquaintance of mine named Cynthia told me a funny story about her boyfriend. They were seeing each other exclusively, and one night he went to a strip-bar. She was not a happy camper and wanted to discourage him from going again. She did not nag. A couple of days later, she pretended that she had gotten a job at a local strip club. "Checking coats. Isn't that great?" Then she talked about finding the right platform shoes.

On their next date, she wore hot pink lipstick and teased her hair as though she'd been electrocuted. Then came the light blue eyeshadow on the entire lid, all the way up to the eyebrow. He wanted to see "hoochies" and girlfriend delivered a "super-deluxe hoochie" package.

It didn't take long before he came unglued: "I don't want my woman in a place like that!" This began a discussion that ended in a mutual agreement that they would both stay out of "places like that." (See? Why argue your case when you can get him to argue it for you?)

There are times when a serious issue arises, and there is a need for a more serious discussion. If and when this situation presents itself, there is still a way of emphasizing your position *without* nagging or repeating yourself several times. If he asks, "Is something wrong?" take a breath and respond calmly. "Yes, something is wrong, but I'd like to talk about it later. I really don't want to talk about it now."

Instead of being muted, the volume is now turned up and the surround-sound is on. Chances are you won't have to say a word because by the time you do get around to discussing it, he's already made sure he won't do it again. Meanwhile, he's thinking of ways to make it up to you. All before you've said one word. Better, no?

It's like he's defragmenting his hard drive. You're making him clean up his own hard drive without any nagging whatsoever. You walk away and do your own thing . . . while he is "self-correcting" himself.

ATTRACTION PRINCIPLE #64
He'll forget what he has in you . . .
unless you remind him.

A lot of women think they need to "cattle prod" the guy out of his oblivion by nagging. "I'll sting him." Or they don't realize that they're nagging.

Every now and then remind yourself: "Hey, men are people too." And put yourself in his shoes—being around someone who acts like your mother isn't a whole lot of fun.

It's with your behavior, not with your words, that you let him know where you stand.

After all, a strong woman is everything men dream and fantasize about. Baseball, hot dogs, apple pie, and . . . bitches—it doesn't get any better than that.

7

THE OTHER TEAM'S

Secret

"PLAYBOOK"

Things You Suspected but Never Heard Him Say

> "Don't learn the tricks of the trade. Learn the trade."
>
> —ANONYMOUS

What Men Think about How Women Communicate

Women often assume that men aren't "in touch" with their feelings and don't have a clue about what is going on in romantic relationships. Because men aren't as likely to express themselves, women presume men "just don't get it."

Men have an aversion to talking about feelings. They even avoid watching movies about "feelings." Mike described to me how men view emotional movies that women like: "There is always a mother, a daughter, and the mother's best friend. The whole movie they are at a beach, or they are squeezing tomatoes in a garden with a stupid straw hat on. And everyone is whimpering the whole time. 'Mama? Boo, hoo, hoo.' Then the mom starts crying. A bunch of women whimpering is not a plot. I can't sit through two hours of that."

Men are about as interested in talking about feelings or watching "chick flicks" as we are watching them get under a car and rebuild an engine. To them, watching a movie like *Terms of Endearment* or *Steel Magnolias* is cruel and unusual punishment. One guy named Chris recalled: "It was horrible! And I had to watch that shit for three hours just to prove that

I wasn't an asshole." This statement even brought support from a guy standing nearby: "I feel for you, man. That sucks. That's almost as bad as having to listen to Michael Bolton. All that wailing and weeping? I can't listen to it."

What is also interesting is how men discuss "feelings." If you ask a man to say that word out loud, he'll pronounce it with a tone of dread. "*Fff-fffff—feeeee-*lings." As the conversation continues, you'll notice a pained facial expression as if he's "going in" for some kind of invasive surgical procedure. Side effects vary; usually digestive problems occur. (Therefore, before discussing "feelings," make sure to steam some rice to quell his upset stomach.)

This lack of sentiment leads women to believe men are "out of touch." But nothing could be further from the truth. I spoke with hundreds of men of all ages while researching this book. The youngest was eighteen and the oldest was seventy; some were married and some were single. To my surprise, they were more articulate about their perceptions than any girlfriends I've ever talked with were about theirs. I found the men to be surprisingly forthcoming and truthful.

In the balance of this chapter, I've taken the best, most revealing quotes and put them all together in list form to help women learn what men notice. I've highlighted the quotes that reveal what men think about a needy woman, a feisty woman, and what turns men on or off.

This information will "connect the dots," confirming the advice given in the other chapters. You'll understand not only what the advice is, but also, *why the advice throughout this book* was given.

The Top Fifteen Signs That a Woman Is Needy

1. "If a woman doesn't wear her heart on her sleeve, she comes off as less emotional and more appealing. It makes the relationship go smoothly. For example, a guy *has* to go to work. It isn't that he doesn't want to spend time with a woman; it's that a lot of times he *can't*. So when a woman gives you room to live your life without getting upset, you'll feel she's adding much more to your life."

2. "I like a woman who's quiet at times because then you're not sure what she's thinking. She'll seem more secure with herself, like she has control over herself and her emotions. You want to be with a person who can think before she speaks."

3. "Some women seem defensive or guarded, and that can be viewed as insecurity, also. There was one woman who turned me off before we even went out. She was so concerned about *protecting* herself that she told me what she wouldn't tolerate in our first phone conversation. She gave me this warning based on what happened with the *last* guy. We hadn't even had our first date, and already she was laying down the law. I hadn't even made a traffic violation and she'd already sentenced me to death. All I did was ask her out on a date!"

4. "I went out with a woman who interrogated me. I got the impression that she had been burned. Actually, it was more like she'd been *scorched*. No guy wants to feel

like he's paying for some other guy's mistakes."

5. "I dated a woman who loved to talk and talk. We'd fall asleep talking, and I'd wake up and she'd still be talking. I realized that she wasn't doing it because she wanted to tell me anything, she was doing it because she just couldn't shut up."

ATTRACTION PRINCIPLE #65
**Many women talk a lot out of nervousness—
which is something that men
will often perceive as insecurity.**

6. "One woman I dated was really needy. She needed constant reassurance about everything. Her family, her friends, and her job. *During sex,* she said to me, 'Do you know what happened to me today at work?' That one killed my ego!"

7. "The conversation is part of the companionship, but it isn't everything. Women overdo talking about feelings. If it feels like you've run out of things to talk about, that's not a good thing. There has to be a balance somewhere in between."

8. "One woman tried to change me. She tried to get me to talk about my 'feelings' more. Hey, look. I can deal with my *own* problems."

9. "When someone tries to get me to open up and I don't want to, there is no way they are getting the information out of me. I'll close up even more. I don't

need a woman to 'help' me."

10. "It really makes us happy when a woman lets us go out with the guys and has no attitude about it. Like if I get tickets to a hockey game at the last minute. If she's cool even when I cancel plans with her, it wins my respect. It feels like she is secure with herself, and she cares about what makes me happy, too."

11. "I had one girlfriend who talked so much I could walk away into another room and she'd still be talking. One time I was in the bathroom trying to have some privacy and she was talking to me through the crack of the door. I really think there was something wrong with her."

ATTRACTION PRINCIPLE #66

Talking about feelings to a man will feel like *work*. When he's with a woman, he wants it to feel like *fun*.

12. "When a guy talks about something, it's over in thirty seconds. But for a woman, it goes on and on. What seems like a trivial thing to him seems like it's life threatening to her. So then you try to help and you say, 'Honey, it doesn't matter.' But that makes it worse because she thinks you don't care."

13. "I think a woman who talks less is more attractive because it makes her more mysterious. It is not a good thing to just ramble on. Communication should be

about quality not quantity. If a woman is uncomfortable or bothered, he should be able to feel it without her saying a word."

14. "One woman wanted the two of us to always be together. She tried to change how I spend all my time. And every guy has his own special time or recreation. She wanted me to do stuff I didn't want to do. If she knows I am not the 'artsy' type, she should let me be who I am. She shouldn't be dragging me to an art gallery or a museum. If a guy treats a woman well, but he doesn't write poetry or buy stupid cards expressing his *feelings,* she should just leave well enough alone."

15. "I don't mind a woman who changes the decor in the house, but when she is obsessed with changing me, it gets old. I want a woman who has a sense of purpose in her own life, so she doesn't waste all her energy trying to control mine."

What you can glean from this feedback is that, no matter how much a woman wants intimacy, she can't force it out of a man—much less change his stripes. Notice that in the last quote, the man even says the woman is *wasting her time.* Whenever a woman speaks in language that appears in any way emotional, most men will immediately discredit it and think of it as "girlie babble." Keeping it short and to the point is essential, otherwise he won't hear a single word.

Not only this, but constantly trying to force a man to talk about feelings or pay an inordinate amount of attention to your feelings is counterproductive. Here's why:

ATTRACTION PRINCIPLE #67
**Forcing him to talk about feelings all the time
will not only make you seem needy, it will eventually
make him lose respect. And when he loses respect,
he'll pay even less attention to your feelings.**

Therefore, if you feel as if he's ignoring you, be "dumb like a fox." When he isn't meeting your needs, just pull back slightly and don't explain a thing. As explored in the last chapter, men don't respond to words.

Women chase men by trying to force-feed conversations about feelings. And predictably, they run. In order for the child to run to Mommy, Mommy has to first stop chasing the child.

If, however, you're not *demanding* it, or chasing it, or trying to inflict "cruel and unusual girlie babble," you'll have his respect. Whenever you keep your piece short and sweet and pull back in a slightly mysterious way, you'll appear more dignified and he'll pay much more attention to what you feel—without any words at all.

The Top Fifteen Reasons Men "Play It Cool"

I asked men why they hide their feelings, or "play it cool." I asked why they often put up pretenses that they are cool, "macho," and tougher than they feel. They do this because they feel they have to, *especially* when dealing with women.

Women often wonder why men take so long to make a phone call. For example, a man asks for her phone number and then waits six days before calling. Then he takes her out on a really fun date and waits another five days before calling again. Meanwhile, she's scratching her head and asking, "What's up with that?"

Men are used to being turned down by women so this delaying tactic is how they keep their guard up. In the beginning, he'll be calculated. He'll be rational as opposed to "emotional," because to him appearing too obvious, or "emotional," will be perceived as a sign of weakness. On Tuesday, he'll say to himself, "I think I'll call her on Thursday." Most men don't have a clue that the woman would have preferred a call on Tuesday.

So why do they do it? They do it to "save face" and to give the impression they're "in control" of the situation. An attractive guy by the name of Steven surprised me with his candor. He said, "You have to approach women looking like you do it all the time, and it isn't a big deal to you. The minute you act like it's important to you, the woman smells it and she treats you differently." This is the reason men will wait before calling and then act a little bit cavalier. *They believe that women disrespect men who appear weak or vulnerable.*

What you can take away from this is: *Do not take it personally* if he doesn't call for a day or two. Often when it seems as though he's slightly rejecting you, it can be a compliment in disguise; he wants you *so much* that he doesn't want to appear too obvious about it. Other times men pull back deliberately to see what your reaction will be, because they are curious to see how much *you* care. If you don't believe me, keep reading. Here's what these sneaky devils copped to:

1. "Guys want women to think they have other options with women, even when they don't. So they exaggerate. They do it to make themselves look more attractive to a woman."

2. "Sure, men play cool. Because they think the woman is going to find them more attractive or appealing. I know some guys that check out a woman who isn't even that beautiful, just to make his girlfriend a little insecure."

3. "Guys don't want to admit it to themselves that one woman can have that kind of control over them. It deflates our egos to think that women can affect us that much. We don't want to feel like we have no control over ourselves."

ATTRACTION PRINCIPLE #68
In the beginning, the only thing you need to pay attention to is whether he keeps coming around, because he'll only be able to suspend or hide his emotions for so long.

4. "I may not call a girl too much in the beginning because I don't want to give the impression that I'm too eager."

5. "Guys are just as emotional as women are. They just don't show it because society says you aren't supposed to. As a guy, you have to appear to be in control of yourself."

6. "When she acts like she doesn't care, it can scare you. Women can crush men and they don't even know it. If a woman puts her foot down and walks away? It can crush a guy . . ."

7. "If a man is really falling for a particular woman, a lot of times he'll try to conceal it. Very few men will ever break down and cry over a woman in front of her."

8. "Of course men play cool . . . to get women interested in us. We want women to like us and don't want them to think we are too eager. If you show you're too interested right off the bat, women will think you are desperate."

9. "Sometimes I'll pretend to ignore a woman in the beginning, or I won't call as much to keep a woman's interest. No guy wants to look too desperate."

10. "Men are needier sexually. Women can control their sex drives, whereas men are controlled by theirs."

11. "Guys do it to appeal to women. Most guys believe that nice guys finish last and that women on some level want a bad boy."

12. "If you appear weak, people take advantage of you. Some men think if you open up too much, a woman will use it against you."

13. "If you let a woman know that you haven't been in the company of a woman recently, she could get the impression you're desperate or just trying to be with any woman."

14. "Women are in control, because they control the sex. In fact, women have a lot more control than they know. A lot of guys feel like this puts us at a disadvantage."

15. "When a guy plays cool, he thinks he's impressing the woman with his power or his strength. He's just trying to be hip, like he knows what's up. No guy wants to be perceived as a Mommy's boy or a wimp."

ATTRACTION PRINCIPLE #69
**Men treat women the way they treat other men.
They "play it cool" because they don't want
to appear weak or desperate.**

The Top Fifteen Male Views on Keeping the Romance Alive

A number of men also spoke to me about keeping the passion alive, particularly those who are married or have been married. During this part of the interview, I always felt like it was a word game. I said "romance," and they thought *sex.* I said "passion," and they thought *sex.* I said "new experiences," and they thought about *sex.* I said, "variety," and they responded with a question, "You mean *sex,* right?" Given this, the most obvious thing men would want a woman to take away from a conversation on the subject of how to keep the passion alive is with respect to . . . you guessed it . . . *sex!* While men are less likely to talk about feelings, they still need to feel connected with the person they are in love with and it's equally important for them to keep the magic "spark." When a man stops having sex, he starts to doubt his manhood, and his desirability gets called into question. It isn't just about the physical act.

1. "A guy needs to always feel that he's desirable to his wife or girlfriend. We need that feedback."

2. "Do something different in bed. Anything. As long as it's different than what he's used to. The element of surprise is a turn-on. If you always get on top, do it sideways."

3. "Late in the evening you're so exhausted. The daily grind can really take the passion out of a relationship. You have to make the time for each other. Go out for a dinner and get a babysitter if you have to."

4. "People use the excuse of money, time, being away from the kids to stop being intimate or romantic. It's really important to keep the passion."

5. "Men like a woman to be creative so it doesn't get stale. If she's too predictable because you talk about the relationship all the time instead of going out and having one, he'll get bored quickly."

6. "Recently, my wife and I started leaving the kids with family once a month and we go away for a Friday night or a Saturday night. It keeps the romance alive. It's the adult conversation one-on-one."

7. "It's easy to say, 'We can't afford to eat out.' Or, 'We can't afford to go away for the weekend.' The bills may be racking up or you feel like you should spend the money on the kids. But you really can't afford to give up the romantic things or your sex life. It's also very important."

ATTRACTION PRINCIPLE #70
**The element of surprise both inside and outside
of the bedroom is important to men,
and it adds to the excitement.**

8. "Anything that surprises a guy will add excitement. It's about having new experiences with someone."

9. "If a guy keeps getting turned down sexually, eventually the passion will die. Guys want sex a minimum of a couple of times a week, and ideally, they want a woman who doesn't have to be asked."

10. "Just once I would like to have a woman take my hand and lead me to the bedroom. Guys *always* have to be the aggressors. We *always* have to do the work to get a woman 'in the mood.' Sometimes guys just don't want to have to work that hard."

11. "I like a woman who takes the initiative sexually from time to time. Maybe not the first time, but definitely when you are in a relationship. It makes him feel like you want him more."

12. "I think it keeps the romance if you have time apart even when you're living together. It is important to be able to do stuff alone and not have her give you a hard time about it. When I go fishing, I find that I really miss my wife. And that's a *good* thing, isn't it?"

13. "Sometimes a woman can make a guy feel important by asking questions or expressing an interest in what he likes. They can try something new together that they wouldn't normally do. I'd suggest planning a weekend

away with him that you can both look forward to."

14. "The weekends can be filled with a lot of busywork. Shuttling the kids around or doing housework. I think it can help keep the romance to do some of the mundane things apart from one another. Sometimes in the morning I can take the kids while she does chores, and then she can take the kids out while I stay at home and do certain duties. In the evenings you have a better time being together. I don't need to see my wife cleaning the floors with a bandana on."

15. "It's comforting if you've been with someone awhile to do the same three tricks in bed that you know they like. But it becomes routine after awhile. Throw in a change-up or a curve ball. It doesn't have to be outrageous, just something you don't normally do."

ATTRACTION PRINCIPLE #71
Don't always do the same thing over and over in the bedroom. Vary it so that it doesn't become a predictable routine.

The Top Fifteen Things That Turn Men Off

There were just a few miscellaneous comments men had about other things that put them off. This section may be self-explanatory to some, while others may find these things not so obvious. In any event, since your man is not likely to say these things directly, you might want to make a small mental note of the following:

1. "A woman should always keep the bathroom door closed when she's on the toilet. I think it's really disgusting to watch a woman on the toilet. And don't leave feminine pads and stuff around for the guy to look at, either. We don't even like it when we see douche commercials on TV."

2. "I get a little turned off by a woman who is too materialistic. If she pays attention to what kind of shoes I'm wearing or what kind of watch I have on or what kind of car I drive, I'll back off."

3. "When a woman is jealous, it can be a turnoff. One time I was on a date and this person with long blonde hair was in the car next to us. My date accused me of checking her out. It turned out to be a guy!"

4. "Mystery is important. I was on the phone with a woman and the first time we spoke she said that she was going to lose weight so we could have sex. How much does a guy need to be talked into having sex?"

5. "I don't like a woman who doesn't have a life, or a job. Or messed-up credit. Or an old boyfriend who's a nut case. I like a woman who is responsible."

6. "I like a woman I can see without any pressure involved. If a guy is under a lot of pressure and she adds to it, he'll immediately shut down."

7. "I don't like it when a woman makes me look bad in front of people. If I do something wrong, she should

bring it up at home."

8. "When he walks in the door after a long day, let him do his own thing for a half-hour. Acknowledge his presence and give him a kiss and don't immediately drop what you need on him."

9. "A woman shouldn't let a guy know she is centering her world around him. One girl told me she spent three hours getting ready to meet me for the first time. That's a little too much."

10. "The fear every guy has is that after marriage the girl is going to cut her hair off, gain a bunch of weight, and stop putting out."

11. "No woman who wants to be involved with a halfway decent guy should ever get drunk with him. If you're home drinking and you get a buzz, that's one thing. If you're at a bar and you make an idiot of yourself, it's a total turnoff. No one likes to be with a drunk."

12. "Never let a guy know you're sitting home waiting for his call, or that he's your whole life. He also likes knowing other men want you, just as long as you aren't sleeping with any of them."

13. "When a woman chases you, it will turn you off. I remember when the sorority girls would come over to the fraternities. In a way, I felt like the cows were coming to graze on our turf. It was too easy."

14. "It's like punching a clock when you're with a woman who makes you feel like you have to report back to her. That's an instant turnoff. "

15. "A woman should never show up *unannounced,* both at a guy's house or at his work. He'll instantly think of her as a 'fatal attraction' type."

The Top Fifteen Reasons Men Prefer a Feisty Woman

Women are almost brainwashed since kindergarten that they should be *nice*. Just think about the nursery rhyme that says girls are made of "sugar and spice and everything *nice.*" Pop culture does not encourage women to be feisty, so women get the idea that being nice, and agreeable is the winning ticket. It's good to be nice. It's when a woman feels she has to be nice independent of how she is treated that there's a problem. It often means the woman is nice at the expense of being self-abnegating.

As you've read throughout these chapters, a man will often be turned off by a woman who *doesn't* stand her ground. When you read the following quotes, this message should come full circle, since now you will be hearing it directly from men: They are secretly turned on by a bitch, or a woman who *will* stand up for herself. At this point we are getting to the meat and potatoes of the "Other Team's Secret Playbook." Here's where men—in their own words—disclose why they are turned on by bitches. This is one of their best-kept secrets of all.

1. "When you banter with a woman and she can give it right back to you, it's a turn-on."
2. "I like a woman who can put me in my place. If I'm being a jerk and she brings it to my attention, it makes me respect her."
3. "The childlike qualities in us [men] propel us to try to take advantage. It's a good thing to know the woman you love won't put up with it."

4. "Yes, I admit it. Sometimes I start a fight with my wife. It isn't that I deliberately want to give her a hard time; it's just that sometimes I have a hard day and misery loves company. When she puts me in my place, it makes me respect her."

5. "I like a woman who won't play games. Her confidence says that she must know something I don't. Then I say to myself, 'Hey, she *must be* worth keeping.'"

6. "When a woman is always really sweet and nice, it can become monotonous."

7. "If a guy thinks a woman is stupid, he won't take her attention that seriously because he doesn't respect her opinion. If she's really smart and appears to have her act together, I am more flattered that she wants to be with me. I feel like I have something of value."

ATTRACTION PRINCIPLE #72
Most men tend to disrespect a woman who appears to be too *malleable*.

8. "When you try to get away with doing something you know isn't right and a woman says, 'I don't have time for that,' it can be a turn-on. It depends on the situation, but I like a woman who has the integrity to stand by what she believes."

9. "She is so sexy to me when she has that spiciness about her. She isn't afraid to disagree or tell me what

she thinks. She doesn't always kiss my ass and that keeps me on my toes."

10. "She didn't take anything lying down. I complained at the time, but I admit this turned me on."

ATTRACTION PRINCIPLE #73
Don't be afraid to stand up for yourself or speak your mind. It will not only earn his respect, in some cases it will even turn him on.

11. "I like a woman to put me in my place, if I know I deserve it. What is sexy is when a woman is comfortable enough with her own power. Or when she isn't so timid or afraid to rock the boat."

12. "A man respects a woman who won't tolerate being treated badly."

13. "I treat women as equals, so I like to compete in a fun way with my wit. I like a woman who mentally challenges me in a fun way by bantering with me, or with her sense of humor. It can be competitive in a playful kind of way."

14. "I actually like a woman with a little bit of a temper. Because then I know she won't let me take advantage of her. Pride is sexy."

15. "A woman who is feisty is sexually stimulating. You assume she'll be wilder. With a nice girl, you are afraid she'll run home and tell her mommy what you did to her."

ATTRACTION PRINCIPLE #74
Men often automatically assume that a bitchier woman will be more assertive in bed, and that a nice girl will be more timid.

The Top Ten Ways to Tell Whether a Man Is in Love

Since men are so good at hiding the way they feel, a woman often wonders how she can tell whether a man is in love with her or just "going through the motions." Here is the most important thing to remember when asking yourself this question: If you have to second-guess whether he loves you, and you've been together for a very long time, you might be settling for less.

What the men shared with me is that it's often the little things a man will do for a woman that are most telling.

1. "You know a guy's in love when it's a Monday night and she says, 'Why don't we do this?' and he does. He's in love when he starts to regularly pick her over his friends."

2. "When he seems to be overjoyed. Suddenly he's really happy and he seems different. When he suddenly appears more alive to his friends and family."

3. "You know a guy is 'in deep' when he'll let the girl keep feminine stuff in the house. Suddenly he's proud to have feminine decor. He'll buy the furniture that she likes. And he'll let her keep tampons under his sink.

He'll want her in his life in every way."

4. "He'll start taking better care of himself, and he'll start to think about long term. Financially, physically, and in every other way."

5. "He'll go out of his way [for her]. He'll fly to see her. If she has a craving, he'll get out of bed to get her a doughnut in the middle of the night."

6. "Men are into variety until they fall madly in love. If he really wants one woman, it doesn't matter who else he can have because he wants to be with *her*. Other women aren't a threat when he's attached. A lot of temptations go away when you really fall hard."

7. "When he thinks about her all the time, when he does thoughtful things for her, or when he's always thinking of ways to please her."

8. "Suddenly, he feels like he can stop looking around the corner for someone else."

9. "When he's willing to do something out of character to please her. He never thought of having children or getting married, but with this woman he is willing to do all of the above."

10. "She won't have to ask. She'll just know it in her gut."

ATTRACTION PRINCIPLE #75
When a man falls in love, suddenly he'll go out of his way and think nothing of it. He'll do things for *this* woman he wouldn't have done for anyone else.

Much of the advice given in this book has been based on the admissions men have made to me. At one point, I asked a doctor named George why he won't share this secret information with his partner. He answered, "Because with you there is no consequence. But with her there *would* be a consequence." The consequence George is speaking of is a loss of power for men. In other words, *the attraction a man has for a feisty or bitchy woman is rarely something he'll want her to know about.*

I knew the information the men were giving up was not only truthful but also very loaded, because there was such a "hush, hush" quality to it. Men would regularly ask me not to use their names because they said that other men would feel betrayed by what they had disclosed.

Obviously, it's helpful to know how men think. But the information in this chapter isn't intended to give you ways to work *even harder* to appease a man. The nice girl does that already, to a fault. If there are two eggs in a frying pan, she'll take the broken yolk for herself. If she bakes two cookies and one breaks, she'll keep the broken one and give him the good cookie. The nice girl has no idea why overcompensating backfires when it's done day-in and day-out. She doesn't realize that she becomes so involved in him that she loses herself, and in the process, she risks losing him as well.

Refer to the Top Fifteen Lists in this chapter again and again, but don't take the information and work *even harder* to please your man. Instead of working so hard to please him, work harder to please yourself . . . because ultimately, this is what will truly please him.

8

KEEPING YOUR
Pink
SLIP

The Reasons That Holding Your Own
Financially Gives You Power

"Elegance does not consist of
putting on a new dress."

—COCO CHANEL

Financial Independence: Who Has the Title on You?

There's one aspect of holding your own in a relationship that cannot be overlooked: money. Many women dream of having a knight in shining armor pay all the bills. The part they don't show is what happens after Prince Charming sweeps you off your feet. If he's paying all the bills in the castle, he'll also be calling the shots. That is when the princess stops feeling like a princess and starts feeling like a servant.

This chapter explores what happens when you give up your "pink slip" and the ability to provide for yourself.

ATTRACTION PRINCIPLE #76
He'll never respect you as being able to hold your own unless you can stand on your own two feet financially.

When you have the clear title on a vehicle, you are the legal owner and you have the "pink slip," or certificate of ownership, to it. The "Pink Slip" in some states means you've been fired. However, the meaning here pertains to *ownership of a vehicle*. When you have the pink slip, there are no lien-holders. There are no monies owed. There are no debts unpaid. This means you own it *free and clear,* so what you do with that vehicle is entirely up to you. Likewise, when a woman keeps the pink slip over herself, she gains leverage in the relationship.

This is what many mothers tell their daughters: If a woman gives up her independence and becomes financially dependent on a man, she'll have far fewer choices in life. She'll end up at someone else's beck and call. She'll be at *someone else's mercy.* This is why a woman should maintain her independence, her "pink slip," and full ownership of *herself.*

Work = Money = Keeping your pink slip = The ability to choose the way you want to be treated = Dignity

What mothers may or may not elaborate on is how a man feels about a woman when he has to carry her financially. Before long he'll feel as though she's an added responsibility instead of an asset. At that point, he'll stop viewing her as a privilege to be with.

This doesn't apply to a woman taking care of children. When a family is involved, no doubt she will be doing her part . . . and then some. He won't perceive her as dead weight, because he knows her job can sometimes be harder than his. In this case a father recognizes that he prefers his job over hers, so he can't help but *respect her* for her work.

As long as you have the resources to choose your terms, you keep your pink slip and you keep your power. If you choose to leave, you can always grab a suitcase and go. This very independence makes him *not want you to leave.*

All the "feistiness," or "sexiness," or bitchy attitude in the world won't change a man's awareness that you cannot hold your own with respect to your livelihood.

Once you hand over that pink slip, he feels trapped because you've now become a *responsibility,* rather than a privilege. And that feels like something he is *stuck* with. He has to provide food for two, housing for two, and pay all the other bills for two. It doesn't take long for him to feel the added pressure and the doubled responsibility of carrying not only himself but also another person.

A bitch will usually maintain her independence and contribute to the relationship in some way because her pride won't allow her to be perceived as a burden on someone else. And she won't put herself in a position where she can't rock the boat, which she *will* do if and when she feels that she isn't being regarded highly enough.

It's important to let him know you place your dignity above all else, even if you're dating a very successful man. He has to feel that, if he mistreats you, you'll pack up and move out of his mansion into a one-bedroom without any hesitation. He has to feel you'll drive a Pinto rather than a Mercedes Benz, if it means you'll be tolerating disrespect. He has to know you'll give up a comfortable lifestyle before you'll accept being misused or mistreated.

Usually this can be conveyed with actions, but sometimes it can be expressed with words. For example, let's say you're watching the TV movie *The Burning Bed* in which Farrah Fawcett plays an abused woman who, in every other scene, is sporting a new black eye. You can use this as a tender "lovey-dovey moment" in which to express your *Terms of Endearment* for your man, while eating popcorn. Simply turn and look at him, gaze into his eyes and say, "I would sooner be flipping burgers at McDonalds."

ATTRACTION PRINCIPLE #77
You have to show that you won't accept mistreatment. Then you will keep his respect.

When faced with an independent woman, a guy is too busy trying to keep his "welcome" to get bored. But with a financially dependent woman, he thinks he can slack off and *she'll take it*. Even if he isn't the type to mistreat a woman, he'll grow bored if he gets the sense that she'll take whatever he dishes out.

You don't have to be rich; you just have to maintain the ability to take care of yourself. This directly relates to whether he's respectful at all times. He can't buy you a dinner because you're hungry. It has to be a gift that he chooses to give and that you choose to receive. Then the gifts keep coming.

Jeanette told me about how her ex-husband had made her feel when he was the only one working. She recalled:

He was a surgeon and made a lot of money. But for four years, I didn't own a coat. I felt that I couldn't justify spending a couple of hundred dollars on a good coat when I wasn't bringing any money in. So I would wear jackets that I had owned since high school, or I would borrow his coats. The minute I went out and got a part-time job, I felt so much better about myself. Not only because I could buy things, but because I didn't have to ask him for everything.

If you can take care of yourself, everything he gives you becomes gravy. He isn't providing the whole meatloaf. The whole four courses. He doesn't provide you with your livelihood.

ATTRACTION PRINCIPLE #78
Your pink slip is maintained when you can stand on your own—with him or without him. He should never feel that you are completely at his mercy.

Susan B. Anthony said, "I never felt I could give up my life of freedom to become a man's housekeeper." It *isn't* about whether a woman is a man's housekeeper or whether she's bringing in "dollar for dollar" that's important. And it also isn't about whether she stays at home to raise children, because this is even harder work. The variable is this: Whether a woman *has the resources or ability to leave if and when she wants to go.*

When a man financially supports a woman completely, one of two things will happen:

1. He'll begin to feel "locked in," or trapped in a dead-end situation.
2. He'll begin to view her as a little girl.

ATTRACTION PRINCIPLE #79
**When a man views a woman as a "little girl"
or a sister he has to take care of,
the passion diminishes. He doesn't want to
make love to his sister.**

Again, a man wants a strong woman, not a helpless little kid. Sexually, this will impact the float in his boat.

I know one couple in which the husband, Michael, is the breadwinner. They have no children, and he pulls all of the financial weight. Every time his wife, Nancy, walks in the house with a new pair of shoes, she gets the "two feet" speech.

The Two Feet Speech

"You only have two feet. Why do you need so many shoes? There are 365 days in a year. You have 100 pairs of shoes. That's one pair of shoes for every 3.65 days. I have flip-flops, sneakers, and a couple of pairs of work shoes. Why do you need so many shoes? Do you see these shoes I have on? I have worn these every day for the past two years. I don't understand. Why do you need so many shoes?"

If she were working, would he give her this speech? Not likely. But if a man pays all the bills, the "money gets funny and the change gets strange." Better for her to be a waitress at Denny's one day a week, and he won't say a word. She would put on her new shoes, strut her stuff, and not have to explain "nothin' to nobody."

ATTRACTION PRINCIPLE #80

The ability to choose how you want to live, and the ability to choose how you want to be treated are the two things that will give you more power than any material object ever will.

When he views you as a little girl, he may do things that demonstrate his loss of respect. He may assign you an "allowance" or tell you how much money you can spend. Or he'll tell you what you can or cannot buy. All of these restrictions reflect your loss of freedom and a loss of your ability to make your *own* choices. Here's why this is relevant:

- The ability to remain an independent thinker is what keeps his interest and the mental challenge.
- The ability to make your own choices in life is your most important tool. It is the very thing that gives you power.

Not only will he tell you what you should have, the man who is paying all the bills will eventually begin to tell you what you like or don't like as well. He won't ask for your opinion, he'll *tell* you what your opinion should be. It sets you up to be treated like a Barbie doll that he can control. Then the following will occur:

- He'll begin to think that he's entitled to the last word.
- He'll behave as if what he says goes.
- He'll have control over your happiness and sadness.

- You'll be treated as though he's the boss and you're the subordinate.
- He may offer his help on his own terms, and you'll wait at bay.

ATTRACTION PRINCIPLE #81
**In a relationship of any kind,
if one person feels the other person isn't bringing
anything to the table, he or she will begin to disrespect
that person.**

Again, it's not a question of whether he pays most of the bills, it's a question of whether you can still stand on your own two feet, if push comes to shove. Then he doesn't have the title, he's merely leasing with the option to buy. He can feel like the "head of household." Remember, he should feel like the Grand Poo-Bah over his habitat and his domain. But he should never feel that he holds the key to your livelihood.

The ability to take care of yourself ensures that all of the following will remain intact:

1. The mental challenge
2. The respect
3. The longevity of the relationship
4. The sexual desire

A case in point. Roxanne, who could be described as a "gold digger," lived with Kent at his Malibu estate. She drove a Mercedes Benz and made regular shopping sprees on Rodeo Drive. Her survival, her livelihood, and her whole existence were contingent on Kent, a man she didn't particularly care for. Although on the surface she appeared to have it all, she had completely given up her pink slip.

One day, I drove to Roxanne's place to pick her up for lunch. Before we left, she opened a drawer and took out some cash, and said she had to make a quick deposit into her account. She had bounced a check for $20. She then said, "Kent lets me keep my pride. He puts the money in a drawer, so I don't have to ask for it."

In this example, there was no pride to be "kept." Pride is . . . having your own paycheck. There is only one thing better than "With Love" and that is the phrase, "Pay to the order of."

In the above example with Roxanne, there is no question that the problem was financial. Kent even suggested that she get a part-time job. He said, "I'd respect you more if you had a job." Still, she didn't make an effort to look for work. And two weeks later, she was tearfully packing her Gucci bags.

Being a gold digger never pays, as evident by the headline stories on the news. As a matter of fact, gold diggers recently suffered an even bigger setback: *Viagra.* Now she's working twice as hard for equal pay. And no dental benefits.

All a woman has to do to balance the relationship is pay an electric bill with her own money or bring home groceries from time to time. Any of these things express her gratitude; then the man is happy to pay for everything else. He doesn't have to feel it's always equal, just *reciprocal.*

ATTRACTION PRINCIPLE #82
Financial neediness is no different than emotional neediness; in both instances, he can still get the feeling that he has a 100 percent hold on you.

Another woman I know, Michelle, was living with a man for four years. For most of that time, he paid every bill and never complained because Michelle didn't have any money coming in. Then she inherited some money. She had $120,000 sitting idle in a savings account. At that point, he asked Michelle to help pay some bills; she declined.

He didn't ask her to carry all the weight, or even half the weight. He merely asked her to pitch in. The interest from her capital would have been more than enough to show him that she was pitching in for a few bills. Still, Michelle insisted that the money was for "her retirement."

Shortly thereafter, he "retired" from the relationship—at which point she moved out. She was then forced to pay several times the amount of money for her own living expenses. Contributing within her means would have been the right thing to do. It was also the financially advantageous thing to do. But the point is not purely financial. The relationship would have had a better chance of working if she had *balanced things out* by pitching in.

One self-made millionaire named Benji described his perspective: "One thing a successful man learns very quickly is that women respond to his money. They realize that women will line up for a man with deep pockets. All he has to do is show them that he is wealthy or that he drives a nice car and that he owns a big house. And they line up like ducks."

Granted, there are plenty of affluent men who like having an accoutrement or a Barbie doll on their arms who, they hope, will graduate into the esteemed ranks of a "Stepford Wife." But this man is not a "quality catch," and this woman will not have any "staying power." He'll be much more likely to trade in a helpless "dingy" type of woman for a newer model because he sees her as a toy to begin with. What a quality man wants "for keeps" is a strong woman. He wants a partner he respects and one who is worth catching: an *equal*. He may provide more monetarily, and she may be a stay-at-home mother. But she is contributing. In other words, she isn't "on the take" and she can stand on her two feet. This means she is there by *choice*.

ATTRACTION PRINCIPLE #83
Regardless of how pretty a woman is, looks alone will not sustain his respect. Appearance may pull him in, but it is your independence that will keep him turned on.

Dignity and pride aren't about whether you pull money out of a drawer, a sack, or a wallet. It isn't about being given a credit card or pulling cash out of a Versateller. If you have an income, however small, it enables you to:

1. Live by your own rules

2. Move to your rhythm, instead of dancing to the beat of someone else's drum
3. Decide how you want to be treated
4. Choose what you will or will not tolerate
5. Leave if you don't get what you want

Everything in this list is precisely what the bitch values most. She keeps her power in *every* way. And as Henry Kissinger said, "Power is the great aphrodisiac."

Dollars and No Sense

While conducting research for this book, I was surprised to find that, generally speaking, men don't mind picking up the tab on a date. What they do mind is the overriding sense that women act as if they are entitled to it—or as if they *expect* it.

When you act as if you expect something, you make a man feel unappreciated. If he pays, it's always best to help him realize that you took time to notice that he went out of his way, and that you are grateful.

Over and over, men have expressed to me their frustration with women who lack gratitude and those who automatically expect a man to pay. There are some women who, even when it's a man's birthday, will take him out and expect him to pay. There were many men who, when interviewed for this book, shared stories about birthdays or holidays in which their partners still expected them to pick up the tab.

In one instance, a woman invited other people to a birthday party and expected the "birthday boy" to pay for everybody. The bill came and people reached for their wallets at the dinner table. "Oh, no, you guys. Marc will get that," the woman said. (Needless to say, Marc was not too happy.) It was the automatic expectation that made him feel unappreciated.

The same goes for flowers or a gift. Do you act excited and appreciative, or do you barely mumble a thank-you and then put the flowers in water? If he brings you a wilted, week-old bunch of flowers from the supermarket that cost $2.99, hold back. Just muster up a thank you, smile, and put them in water.

If he gives you a gift, don't fess up that you always go back and exchange it, or he'll stop bringing you little tokens of his affection. If you can, exchange it for something similar, then tell him it's the same one he bought you. Say, "It looks different on, huh?" (He'll never know the difference.)

If you want him to give you jewelry, don't ever utter the words "pawn shop." If you pawned jewelry given to you by an ex-boyfriend or husband, never disclose that information to a man you're seeing.

Acknowledgment is very important to men. A man I know, John, once ended a relationship with Kate, a woman he was dating, because he felt she was not grateful for a gift that he gave her. One day, when he was at her place, she asked him to move an old television from one room to the next. It had sentimental value to her because her father had given it to her. Without intending to, he dropped the TV and it broke. He described what happened: "I felt really bad, so I went out and bought her a twenty-six-hundred-dollar entertainment center with an amazing TV and stereo. A week later some friends came over and said, 'Wow! What a nice TV.' Then she said in a sarcastic tone, 'John broke the other one.' I just about fell off my chair."

John left her apartment that evening and never saw her again.

Because men aren't conditioned to express their emotions, women sometimes assume that when men spend their money, it doesn't mean anything to them or they didn't have to do anything to earn it. If a man gives you something, show him the respect he deserves by thanking him for the kindness. If you want to be treated well, you have to *encourage* it by making him feel important and special whenever he does something generous and gracious. Otherwise, he won't have an incentive to do it again.

Vinnie, who is very generous by nature, talked about a woman named Shawna who ordered lobster when they went to an expensive restaurant. He said, "I don't mind that she ordered the lobster, but after that she just picked at it. Then she said, 'I wasn't really hungry, anyway.' That bothered me."

Again, the issue is whether you *act as though you expect or are owed what he gives you,* or whether you appreciate his generosity and kindness. Many men enjoy feeling like the provider, as long as they feel *appreciated for what they give.*

If he opens doors for you, let him know that you admire that, too. Whenever he feels that you admire his masculinity, and his brawn, it makes him feel rewarded. This is a way you can build him up.

Money can also be a telling barometer of where a man is coming from, or what a man's intentions are. One woman I know named Carla dated a man named Guy, who made it very clear that he couldn't afford to pay for dates. Guy always had an elaborate explanation as to why he couldn't pay. Each time they went out, it was a Dutch treat. Nevertheless, he insisted on terms that would be "even Steven." Fair and square. Without exception.

One time Carla accompanied Guy to a bar with several of his friends. To her surprise, he had no problem buying his buddies one drink after another. He paid for two rounds in twenty minutes, dropping $80 on drinks without thinking twice. "Waitress? My buddy Steve wants another Long Island iced tea." It was only that morning he had asked his date to pay $7 for her scrambled eggs and bacon at breakfast.

Needless to say, this showed Carla that Guy didn't have sufficient value for the relationship so she stopped seeing him. Usually when a man insists on splitting a check on the first few dates, he's showing you right up front he doesn't value you or the relationship.

Granted, some women refuse to have a man open doors or pick up a tab. They refuse to be "paid for." A bitch has no problem and no "issues" surrounding being treated well, so she lets a man give—and she allows herself to receive. The nice girl who won't allow herself to be treated to a dinner, deep down usually doesn't want to feel obligated to a man and she knows she will be if he pays for dinner. The bitch has no such complex. She says thank-you politely and graciously. And at no time does she feel guilty or obligated. Nor does she feel compromised in any way.

If he's a student or is truly struggling financially but he still wants to impress you, he'll suggest doing something that costs less. Or he'll suggest doing something that doesn't cost anything at all. He can grab some inexpensive wine and a blanket and take you to a beautiful park. Or, he can get movie screening tickets. Or, he can invite you to a party. If he's absolutely crazy about you, he won't let you pay for the tab or go Dutch.

I know of a female doctor named Susie who was living with a man named George, who was also a doctor. She had just graduated and was doing her residency, so her income was less than that of a part-time nurse. George, on the other hand, was a well-established surgeon and was earning a substantial income.

They lived together in his Hollywood Hills home, which was almost paid off; still he insisted that Susie pay a sizable sum of money for so-called "rent." They also split everything right down the middle: groceries, the electric bill, and so on, with the exception of cat litter and cat food, which Susie was required to buy (since it was her cat).

ATTRACTION PRINCIPLE #84
When a man is very consumed with not being taken advantage of, this is a sign that he's "on the take."

Whereas George earned half a million a year, almost all of Susie's disposable income went toward her student loans. Compare the household expenses as they relate to the income of both people:

- His income is $500,000.
- Her income is $25,000.
- They each pay $25,000.
- The cat lives rent-free.

In this example, George earns twenty times Susie's income, but she's paying half the bills. Not only this, the rent deposits transferred from "Bank of Susie" were paying into the equity of *his* home. What does this prove? That even an educated, brilliant woman like Susie can be *too nice*.

The financial part of any relationship has to be give and take. No one person should be doing all of the giving. If he's taking you to an expensive play or ballet and you don't have time for dinner because he ran late at the office, order some Chinese food and have it ready when he arrives at your front door. If he takes you out to dinner, pick up some movie tickets on your way home from the gym and surprise him.

When he offers to take you out and wants you to plan the evening, take into account *his* preferences as well as your own. For example, Linda insisted that her boyfriend, Benny, take her to a play. Benny is a "man's man" and hates the ballet or seeing live plays. Still, she insisted that she wanted to go. He described the evening: "I gave her my credit card and she got the tickets and rented me a tux. There I am, holding 'wussy' little binoculars with the long stick on one side. It was an affront to my manhood. I could not believe I had spent a fortune and then counted the minutes hoping it would end. That was the last time I let her plan anything with my credit card."

When a man asks you to go on a trip with him, be considerate. If he offers to pay and asks you to make the reservations, consult with him about the price of various hotels and let him decide. Men love to feel that they are "in charge" and that their opinion really counts. (At the very least, pretend.) If he pays for the trip, surprise him and pay to have breakfast delivered to the room. Or take him out to dinner to thank him. Buy him a bright colored shirt if you go somewhere tropical or a warm sweater if you're hitting the slopes. Again, it's all in showing that you respect what he gives. Men, like women, don't want to feel taken for granted.

The same goes for a gift that he gives you. If he gives you something, act excited—even if it's ugly. "I love it!" One girlfriend of mine got a T-shirt from her husband. It looked like a cross between a tie-dye and a paisley print and was so hideous it could scare small children. Even though she hated the shirt, she wore it for him when they were at home, just to make him feel good.

More often than not, women who are too nice err on the side of giving too much. They give to a fault. The woman who is too nice senses that he "needs her" and she runs to his aid like a Red Cross rescue missionary. And she gives—*blindly*.

For example, Abby married an Italian man named Franco to help him get his green card. Somewhere along the line during the staged marriage, he convinced her that he was madly in love with her. He found out she was a vegetarian, so he gave up pasta and ate vegetables. She loved hiking, so he took up hiking. She was "spiritual" and he decided he was "spiritual" too. The couple's interview with the INS was successful and Franco was approved to get his green card. A day later he packed his bags and said, "*Ciao, bella!*" Then he rode off into the sunset. She didn't have an engagement ring, but she did end up with a huge legal bill for their divorce.

I've also seen women who are too nice loan money to men. Usually it's the women who are struggling who don't think twice about handing out their hard-earned money. She'll loan him money to buy a stereo for his car when she needs regular maintenance done on her own. The rule on loaning money? *Don't.*

For example, Cheryl, who fits the profile of a bitch, told me the following story. She had dated Rick a couple of times, but she didn't see him consistently because he traveled a lot. After their third date, he hit her up for a loan. As she describes, "Rick called me from Tahoe and said he had 'an emergency.' He asked me to wire him a thousand dollars to a Western Union office that was on the other side of the river. But then he kept changing his story about what the money was for. One story was it was a child-support payment to some woman named Babs, for a kid he never even told me he had. He said that he would need to board a riverboat to get to the Western Union station across the river. The fee was thirty-five dollars each way. So I said, 'Absolutely! I will wire the money. Hurry up and catch that boat.'"

Rick didn't quite catch on. He called later that evening after his roundtrip boat ride and told her that the money hadn't arrived. Cheryl acted stunned and then insisted profusely that she had, in fact, wired the money. "You really have to watch those money wires. I am going to go right down to that office and see what went wrong tomorrow morning!"

The following day Rick went on a second boat ride to get his "loot" from Western Union. To his complete and utter surprise, no funds were forthcoming.

Obviously, Cheryl had no desire to see him again because it was in bad taste for him to call someone he barely knew and make this request. But she remembers the incident with a certain fondness. "Hey, I figured the fresh air might do Rick some good. And, if all else fails, he can get a job on the ferryboat."

ATTRACTION PRINCIPLE #85
People will show you they have self-respect simply by virtue of the fact that they *want* to carry their own weight.

A bitch is not mean; she just doesn't volunteer for any "joyrides." If the man wants to go on a joyride and extends an open invitation, she can choose not to go. Yes, treat others the way you want to be treated. But, at the same time, expect that the man in your life treats you the same way.

The bitchier woman would never let a man think that she's there because she has "nowhere else to go." Her financial independence is a constant reminder to him, however subtle, that if he makes her "stay" unpleasant, she won't be staying for very long. This ensures that the relationship remains respectful, reciprocal, and kind . . . *to all.*

9

HOW TO

Renew

THE MENTAL CHALLENGE

How to Regain That "Spark"

> "One of the things about equality is not that you be treated equally to a man, but that you treat yourself equally to the way you treat a man."
>
> —MARLO THOMAS

Step 1: Instead of Asking Him to Focus on You, Focus on Yourself

What turns a man on about an independent woman is that she is independent *of him*. When a man is with an independent woman, he feels as though he has an equal partner. When she gives up her everyday activities, he slowly begins to view her as less interesting. Instead of thinking that he's scored a wonderful prize, he now begins to view her as extra weight.

The first thing a woman has to do to get that sexy "spark" back is to *shift her focus and energy back onto herself*. She has to develop interests outside her man, just as she did when he was new in her life. Men often find a woman who has passionate interests and activities of her own to be more exciting. They don't have to be things he's interested in necessarily, just as long she has *interests of her own*.

ATTRACTION PRINCIPLE #86
The more independent you are of him, the more interested he will be.

The story that follows proves my point. Rob, an attractive, successful man who could have his pick of any woman he wanted, was mystified by a most unlikely woman. He describes Laura as a "conservative computer nerd" who wears long pleated skirts. After a few dates, he invited her to go on a cruise. Rob wasn't lacking in the confidence department, and he thought he'd teach Laura how to have fun. He thought he'd "rock her world." Laura said she couldn't go. The reason? She had a preplanned Tupperware party.

Rob told what happened next: "I kept hoping she'd change her mind. I ended up going on the cruise by myself and ended up flying home after one day to see what she was up to. A Tupperware party? It couldn't be. I simply could not believe that she'd pass on an exotic vacation with *me* for a Tupperware party. I figured she had to be seeing some other man. I had to see for myself."

He flew home and dropped by that Saturday evening when Laura's party was supposed to be going on. Sure enough, lo and behold, he was dumbfounded and astonished to find that she was actually having a Tupperware party.

When he showed up, Laura was happy to see him. She invited him in and offered him a finger sandwich. Rob could have just as easily been eating spiny lobster or exotic seafood en route to the Bahamas at that very moment with *any woman* he wanted. Instead, he was nibbling on a soggy little tuna sandwich with a toothpick in it. He could have been watching a world-class Vegas-style show, instead the highlighted entertainment on the agenda was Tupperware containers: Gingerbread-shaped ones, star-shaped ones, and even heart-shaped ones.

Rob still remembers it with disbelief. "There I am

listening to a bunch of cackling women, watching them go AWOL over some plastic bowls. I drank coffee in a fancy teacup with a teeny tiny spoon. I could not believe it. I was thinking, 'No. This cannot be so. I don't hold a candle to a this?'"

Was Laura being mean? Not at all. She just didn't go down the beaten path of giving up her own interests in exchange for something he thought would be better. What blew Rob's mind was that her activity meant more to her than the cruise or being with him. He said, "From that point on, she had my full attention." And the unlikely couple became a hot item.

Rob had put on his best "mack-daddy" show-stopping routine, and Laura *wasn't that impressed*. Unlike the bitchier woman, the nice girl will often appear easily impressed. She'll make her desire to have a relationship much too obvious, which often *invites* mistreatment.

ATTRACTION PRINCIPLE #87
If you make it too obvious that you're excited to get something, some people will be tempted to dangle a carrot in front of your face.

"Getting a life" will make it seem like you are no longer impetuous, or impatient. When you are relaxed, you've taken the "need" out of the equation. You no longer appear needy, which immediately changes the dynamic of a stale relationship.

If you want to renew the challenge, it is imperative to *continue the activities you did before he came on the scene.* He'll notice the very first time you tell him that you can't see him because of something else you have planned. It will catch him off guard—and it will fester.

It really throws men off if the activity appears to be something mundane. In the previous example, it was a Tupperware party; but anything along the lines of knitting, gardening, or pottery will do the trick. Rest assured, his ego won't let him lose out to a sweater, a potted plant, or a mound of clay.

No matter what you choose, as long as you are passionate about something *other than him*, it will draw him back in. Guaranteed. He'll be asking himself the same question he asked himself in the first weeks of dating you. "How could she want to do that, when she could be with me?"

When you will not drop everything to be with him, you'll appear as though you have more going for you. This will remind him of your worth, and invariably, he will begin to come your way.

Step 2: Alter the Routine

It's essential when renewing the mental challenge to *alter the routine* that he's become accustomed to. When the mental challenge is gone, the routine becomes predictable and he is on "automatic pilot." His mind can drift elsewhere because he isn't sufficiently being stimulated by you. So, let's let the stimulation commence, shall we?

As Harry Truman said, "If you can't convince 'em, confuse 'em." How? By altering the pattern completely. Give no attitude and no complaints. Instead of seeing him regularly, make the schedule *random*. *Random* means he shouldn't be able to predict like clockwork when he'll see you next or when he'll hear from you next.

ATTRACTION PRINCIPLE #88
**When you alter the routine, *your not being there*
at times is what will make him come around.
Men don't respond to words.
What they respond to is *no contact*.**

This applies to whether you are dating or married. If you need to renew the mental challenge, alter the pattern. Whenever he seems complacent, just alter the pattern. Single women often make plans based on when the man calls. Married women often wait for a man to come home from work. And single and married women alike regularly wait by the phone for a call.

Tracy is a woman who benefited from altering the pattern in her marriage. She used to feel as though her husband, Allen, took her for granted when he would travel out of town on business. Tracy used to wait for Allen's long-distance call every night, even if it meant giving up her own plans to do so. Predictably, Allen started to behave as if calling her was a chore, as though he was "checking in." Or punching a clock. He'd call around 7:30 P.M. and then rush her off the phone so he could go out for drinks with his colleagues.

Girlfriend decided to rock the boat. How? By staying just outside his reach. When he went on his next business trip, she drove him to the airport and didn't say, "Call me when you get there." For the entire trip, half the time she was there when he called; the other half she couldn't be reached. She was out visiting some girlfriends she hadn't seen in awhile, and didn't rush home to wait for his call.

The first evening that Tracy didn't wait for his call, Allen flipped. His whole orientation changed immediately. He called at 7:30 P.M. and virtually every half-hour after that until 10:30 P.M. He went out, had *half* a drink, and then went right back to his room to call his wife again. Tracy walked in at 10:59; the phone rang at 11:01.

Whereas before it was a chore, now Allen was happy to reach her. She was happy, too, especially when she looked down at the answering machine and saw that it was flashing a big red *9*. (Six messages from him, and three mysterious hang-ups.) And everyone went to bed happy.

Suddenly Allen missed Tracy. Why? Because she had a life of her own outside of their relationship.

Never stop living your life. Take a class. Develop a hobby. Meet people. You are only as interesting as the depths of your *own* interests.

The mere fact that you are content with your life keeps you interesting. You are happy with him or without him and this keeps you . . . just outside his reach.

A textbook example is Ellen, a married woman who felt taken for granted. She regularly cooks dinner for her husband, Sydney, and their two kids. Sydney was the only one working, and he frequently stayed late at the office. Usually he didn't show up for dinner. What upset her most, however, was that Sydney would leave her guessing about his dinner plans, and didn't call if he was running very late. Sometimes she'd reheat his plate three times before he got home.

She had formed a pattern of saying, "The kids need to see you at the dinner table, Sydney." But night after night, she found herself reheating his dinner, long after their kids had gone to bed.

Ellen, like many nice girls, was too tolerant. The bitch, on the other hand, would rearrange the dinner agenda. She would *alter the routine*. In a nice quiet moment, she'd look at her husband and casually say, "Hey sweetie, I can see you aren't going to be home during the week. So, I'm not going to bother to cook for you. If there are leftovers from the kids, I'll put them in the fridge. But it may be better if you picked something up on the way home."

For a few nights he'd pick up some food on the way home. The first night he'd grab some Kentucky Fried Chicken, perhaps. The second night he'd upgrade to a deli. And after the cold pastrami sandwich from the corner deli, he'd have a little Alka-Seltzer to help with the heartburn. It wouldn't be long before he'd be coming home for a home-cooked meal, *happily*. And sliding into home . . . right on time.

Another woman named Sandy told me about how she felt taken for granted when she was on her hands and knees cleaning the kitchen floor, after she had cooked for her husband, Wade. He had just started eating and then he came over to her and said, "It is really inconsiderate of you to clean the floor right now. That stuff stinks. Could you please wait until I'm finished eating?" She resisted the urge to strangle him.

For the rest of the week, Sandy backed off. She spoke to him very superficially and became aloof. He had to ask her, "What's wrong?" a dozen times before she addressed what was on her mind. She went from "worker bee" to "queen bee" in just a few short days.

First stop on Sandy's agenda? A maid. She absolutely insisted on it. Then she addressed some table etiquette. Wade often started eating without her and got up before she ever sat down. She said she didn't cook for two, so that she could eat alone. She also suggested going out to eat sometimes, even if it was to a less expensive place. Then she stuck to her guns. Not only do they now have a maid, they also have "date night" once a week.

In both of these instances, by altering the "dinner agenda," the women let their husbands know without words that they, too, had something to lose. Their actions said: "Either we meet in the middle or we don't meet." (And you won't eat.)

ATTRACTION PRINCIPLE #89
Don't give a reward for bad behavior.

Women often make the mistake of going down the beaten path of catering to a man, even when feeling taken for granted. A perfect example is a woman named Laurie who recently called into my radio show. Laurie is a single mom who doesn't have a lot of money. She ran around for two entire days looking for a special heart-shaped pan in order to bake her boyfriend a cake for Valentine's Day.

Trivia question: Do you think a guy's going to care if the cake is shaped like a heart?

He'd probably have preferred a cake in the shape of a wrench or a remote control. In fact, right around Valentine's Day, and shortly after Super Bowl Sunday, you can get a football-shaped cake at the bakery. All you have to do is take the little football people off, throw an asymmetrical "Happy Valentine's Day" on there. Time expenditure? Reduced from two whole days to twelve minutes.

Any woman who feels taken for granted should definitely ease up on the Betty Crocker efforts. It's true that men say, "A man's love comes from his stomach." But there's nothing in this statement that requires you to cook the food before it ends up in his stomach. The question must then be asked: Who should cook it? So many choices, so little time.

The fortune cookie says, it can be delivered. Or, you can pick it up. He can take you out. He can cook on the six-foot beast of a barbecue that he just "had to have." Think of how much fun it is for him. He can spread out both burgers one on each side of the grill, two feet apart from each other. And the bigger the grill, the more virile he'll feel when using it.

If he suggests using the grill, definitely encourage it. Then offer to do the dishes. When he starts cooking, set the table like the classy lady you are. Put out two paper plates and two Dixie cups, and plastic silverware. No table linens needed—just fold a couple of Bounty paper towels.

It's never too early to invite him to participate in kitchen activities. In fact, I'd suggest engaging him on this issue the first time he comes over to your place. Usually by then you'll have gone out a few times, and there is a comfortable rapport.

Walk him into the kitchen and take him on a nice little "Tour de France." Say, "Here are the glasses . . . here are the cups . . . here are the plates. The drinks are right here. If there is anything else you need, please do not hesitate to help your-self. My home is *your* home."

While you're showing your guest where the drinks are, you'll want to casually add, "I only have one little request. I have a little ant problem and, *uh,* all the dishes need to go directly into the dishwasher." What he doesn't realize is that you've just told him you won't wait on him, and that there's no busboy on the premises. If he wants a drink, you've let him know he's welcome to help himself. If he wants a snack, he now knows where to find it.

Don't try to be the "happy helper." He won't value your efforts when you automatically assume the role of a servant. If, however, you are reciprocating for kindness that he has been consistently extending to you, he'll think of everything you give as a special treat.

ATTRACTION PRINCIPLE #90
He simply won't respect a woman who automatically goes into overdrive to please him.

Sometimes changing the routine is a matter of changing the dinner agenda; at other times, it's a matter of changing the times or dates of your little rendezvous.

A college student named Anita provided a classic example of what happens when a woman doesn't pay close attention to the way the pattern is set up in the first place. *The first symptom will almost always be that you sense you are being put "on hold."*

Anita describes how the pattern was set up. "I saw Dave several times a week. He'd call me on my cell phone after class around 4 P.M. and we'd make plans. He started calling later and later. I'd be on pins and needles all afternoon not knowing if he and I had plans that night. I gave up a lot of activities because he was always keeping me 'at bay.'"

Women like Anita end up "at bay" for the simple reason that they are willing to wait. Once he knows you're waiting he'll make you wait forever. This is when it's time to *alter the routine.*

In Anita's situation, the solution is straightforward. She should make herself less available, and schedule the time he is picking her up at least a day earlier. (Notice that she does not offer to travel to see him.) All she needs to do is ask, "What time were you thinking of getting together?" Dave could respond, "I'll call you tomorrow when I get off work." The trick is not to leave it at that. Simply say, "Gee, I may not be here and I'd sure hate to miss you. Just to be safe, let's pick a time now."

Whether it's early or late, agree to a time the day before the scheduled date. If he insists on "letting you know later," just tell him that your cell phone isn't working, your pager won't be on, or you can't take personal calls at work.

ATTRACTION PRINCIPLE #91
**If he doesn't give you a time,
you don't have a date.**

Sometimes men blame a friend. If you hear anything along the lines of: "My buddy is stopping by tomorrow night. I haven't seen him in a while. I'm not sure how long it's going to take. I can't be rude to him and throw him out." Simply say, "No problem. Have a good time tomorrow night." Then, without showing any "attitude," tell him you'll be available to see him a *different* night. Again, what men respond to is *no contact*.

The alternative is that you waste two hours waiting for a call. That's two hours you can spend going to the gym or doing something else that's important to you. Most professional women, or mothers, or students who juggle busy schedules don't have two hours in the day to *themselves*. But they'll spend that time, without flinching, waiting on a phone call.

Altering the routine means mixing things up. If you call twice a day and he doesn't seem happy to hear from you, call more sporadically and less often. If you generally get together on weekends, tell him you can see him that week on a weekday. This week you can see him Tuesday and Friday. Next week? Thursday and Saturday.

One happily married woman I know named Margaret, shared one of her secrets. She said, "Whenever I feel like my husband is getting a little distant, I'll just take off for the weekend to visit friends or family. I'll let him know Thursday that I'm heading out Friday and that I'll be back late on Sunday. I may call once while I'm gone to let him know where I am. And it never fails . . . he's always his usual, loving self again when I come back home."

Here are a few more suggestions on how to alter the routine:

- If you always call the office to find out when he's coming home, from time to time, don't be home when he gets in.
- Don't tell him your whereabouts for every moment of the day.
- If he calls you on your cell phone, don't always rush to pick up.
- If he pages you, don't call back within thirty seconds. Or, don't call back. Let him get hold of you at home—not when you're out and about.
- If he calls on the phone, don't go out of your way to answer it. Let him leave a message. Or, you if want to be considerate, tell him you won't be around beforehand.
- If you sit by the phone and check your "caller ID" or dial "*69" as if your next breath depended on it, turn the ringer off. Read a book. Rent a movie.
- If you live together, leave and go have some fun. And stay out a couple of hours longer than he expected. If he always expects you home at a certain time, come home a little later.

The second he doesn't know where *his woman* is he'll come looking for you. He's a hunter. He'll pursue you. He has an inborn drive that's very territorial . . . over *you*. But if you try too hard, you won't tap that hunger. He'll be satiated—and that means, you won't leave him wanting more.

ATTRACTION PRINCIPLE #92

Often the best way to adjust or fix the problem is by not letting *him* know it's being fixed. When you alter your availability or change a predictable routine, it will mentally pull him back in.

Step 3: Regain Your Sense of Humor

When you lose your sense of humor in a relationship, it's usually around the time that you become "sprung." This means, you've become consumed with your partner's "every move." And chances are, you're often easily upset by what you *aren't* getting in the relationship.

A sense of humor is a sexy quality. Men may not come out and say it, but they notice when you lose that "edge." In the beginning, you probably bantered with him more and had a quick wit. When the mental challenge goes, so does the sense of humor.

A very effective way to put a man in his place or to keep him in check is with humor. You can let him know in a fun, playful way that your security as a woman doesn't *depend on him*.

A sense of humor is more than just finding something funny to say; it's about a person's composure. It lets people know you are comfortable in your skin. It lets him know you aren't sprung. The goal is not to become a knee-slapping standup comic; that's not effective because it makes it seem like you're trying too hard.

ATTRACTION PRINCIPLE #93
Once you start laughing, you start healing.

It's sexy to be able to banter because humor suggests you're an independent thinker. Not only can you think for yourself, but you can laugh at what you see happening around you. If you verbally play-fight with him a little, it's unlikely that he will perceive you as needy.

When he teases you, it's as if he is asking you, "Still got that edge?" Your sense of humor answers him and lets him know that he isn't always going to call the shots.

Here's a case in point. A girlfriend of mine went on a couple of dates with a guy who criticized the color of her nail polish. She said, "The suggestion department is closed for the evening. But fax your idea tomorrow and we'll file it right over there in the suggestion box." (Then she pointed to the kitchen trash.) These two are still together and he is absolutely crazy about her. To this day, she wears the same nail polish color.

Humor not only defuses a situation, it also makes you come out smelling like a rose. Tom Hanks exemplified this in an interview with Barbara Walters. Paraphrasing what she said, "I don't mean to hurt your feelings, Tom, but you aren't considered a sex symbol." He said, "Yeah, but I embrace that. And I think that makes me kinda sexy." He could have chosen to become defensive. Instead he was disarming.

If you don't become defensive and you laugh things off from time to time, he'll respect you more. This is when you show whether you believe in yourself. For example, he may make fun of the way you parked your car. This kind of joking makes him feel manly. A relaxed aura from a woman who can laugh at herself turns him on because he thinks she'll be entertaining and fun.

It doesn't matter if you're wearing a potato sack. A feisty quality will do it for him more than a black nightie on a woman who behaves as though she is desperate for approval. (Yes, even if you're wearing the thigh highs that cut off your circulation and practically cause you to lose a limb.)

Successful politicians are coached on how to use humor to win people over and show confidence. When Ronald Reagan ran for president, he was asked in a debate about the detriment of being the oldest candidate to ever run for the highest office. His response was "I refuse to exploit for my political gain the *youth and inexperience* of my opponent."

In a relationship with a man, whenever you want to keep him on his toes, banter with him. If he says something a little out of line, just say, "We'll let that one slide." Or, "Why do I put up with this?" Or ask him if he wants one broken leg or two . . .

One woman I know named Darla dated a man who made a complete mess every time he came over. They also had a good sex life. He made a pass at Darla and she playfully snubbed him. Then she walked over to the sink and started doing all his dishes. She said jokingly, "The more time I spend doing dishes, the less time we spend doing 'the deed'." Suddenly, the happy helper started pitching in.

ATTRACTION PRINCIPLE #94
You can get away with saying much more with humor than you can with a straight face.

The man in your life watches you. He watches to see how you stand your ground. He watches to see how you respond when he teases you and when you receive criticism from him or someone else. He'll test the waters, because he wants to see how you fight back. He wants to see if you can *hold your own*.

And while we're on the subject of humor, let us now focus our attentions on the word *bitch*. If that fateful day ever does arrive when he tells you that you are a bitch? Stop, and take a deep breath. Then enjoy the moment. Smile internally as you say to yourself, "Okay. Now I know he *truly* does love me."

10

GAINING
Control
OF YOUR EMOTIONS

Q&A—Letters from Readers

"Never allow someone to be
your priority while allowing
yourself to be their option."

—NINA POTTS-JEFFERIES

Crazy in Love

I often hear men say that all women are crazy or emotionally unstable. Some men even break it down by category. In their view, women range from *mildly* irrational . . . to completely psychotic. Men have been known to get together for a few rounds of golf, or a few beers, and exchange notes on the mental health of their newest acquaintance. "I met a new girl, and she seems like she's in charge of her hormones." Perhaps you've noticed that there's always an ex-girlfriend he speaks of. You know, that one ex who snapped and became possessed by demons, causing the demise of their relationship. Of course, he never had anything to do with it. He was a perfect angel . . . and lo' and behold . . . one day he woke up next to the Exorcist.

Maybe this is why women blame themselves for everything. I've lost count of how many times I have heard from women, "I keep screwing up my relationships. I feel like there's something wrong with me." They get the mental analysis from the boyfriend (the self-appointed therapist) and before long, she's second-guessing herself. "He tells me I am acting crazy. And that I'm not normal. I feel like I'm a little crazy." Then she picks up a two-by-four and beats herself with it. Over and over.

Confident women laugh when they receive ridiculous feedback. If a man were to tell a bitch she was "a little crazy," she would tell him to count his blessings. "That's true, and you are so lucky that I'm a little bit crazy. It could have been much worse because most other bitches are completely psychotic. No telling what they would be capable of doing to you. . . ."

When a woman can laugh at herself, doesn't take these things personally, and has control over her emotions, she seems more "stable," safe, and trustworthy. Now the guy thinks there is a better chance of things working out.

This chapter is designed to help the woman who is nice to everyone . . . except herself. She believes everything negative that happens to her is *her own fault*. To help you control your emotions (or, as men say, "remain in charge of your hormones") it might help to read what other women are experiencing. The following dating scenario might sound familiar . . .

Dear Sherry,

I started seeing this guy and the first few months I thought I had died and gone to heaven. He was romantic and wonderful. He called every day, talked on the phone for hours, and we both said we could see ourselves being together forever. I didn't ask him to promise me the moon; he offered this information. That's why I'm so confused. After we slept together I noticed a change. I wanted to get together more often than he did. Although he had time for his friends, family, and work, he made less time for me. I find myself calling and e-mailing him more and I feel rejected much of the time. Is there something wrong with me?

—Anonymous Nice Girl

Let's go back to that "romantic and wonderful" beginning because this is where the miscommunication started. In the beginning, when a man first meets you, you have to understand—the majority of men see a woman as a hump-toy. It's not that men don't eventually fall in love, because they do. But that happens *later*. Even when you see a man who is married, with a minivan, and a Baby-Bjorn hammock and a newborn swinging off his back . . . that was not what he set out to achieve. At first, the game-plan was to get the woman's clothes off. He's a red-blooded creature with plenty of testosterone. And because of *his hormones* . . . he only has three emotions:

- Crabby
- Hungry
- Horny

Therefore, anything he says in the beginning is said most likely to get the desired result: throw-down in the bedroom. It's verbal foreplay. You wear perfume . . . he opens the car door . . . you tell him you've only had three lovers in your whole entire life (with a straight face) . . . and he tells you he is looking for a relationship and you have all the qualities the other women didn't have. It's a sales pitch.

Here is an analogy. Think of him the way you would a trained animal performing tricks in front of a live audience. Like a seal, or a sea otter at Sea World. When a seal balances a beachball on the end of its nose, he's not trying to demonstrate how well-coordinated he is. And the seal isn't doing the tricks to impress the audience. He's doing it for one reason only: to get a salmon. Same goes for men: If he buys dinner and sends flowers, he's balancing a ball on his nose. Some men do it better than others . . . and some seals can even clap three times while the ball is on their nose. But it's all being done for the same reason: to get a reward. If he wants to get the "treat," he has to do the "trick."

Women say, "I refuse to sleep with a guy who is not interested in a serious relationship." That's ammo for him to use against you. If he saw one episode of *Sex and the City*, he knows that using key phrases about "love and commitment" is a one-way ticket to the bedroom. Men watch that stuff to learn what women want to hear, so they can promise those things. One man named Bradley explained: "Men say very little and women 'grab onto it.' A guy could just be making a simple statement and next thing you know she thinks her dreams are coming true." Men believe that women mislead themselves. He puts ideas in your head, and you do all the rest. As Bradley put it, "Women are in love before they even meet the guy." Now, that doesn't mean he doesn't like you, adore you, and think you are the sexiest thing in his eyes. What it means is that to keep the sex coming, men will mislead you about their level of intended involvement, long-term.

A Hint of Indifference Acts as a Trigger, and Hooks Him

There's a way to get a relationship, but sleeping with the guy right away and announcing you want a "relationship" or allowing him to put a poodle leash around your neck is not the way to go about it. Instead, you have to knock him off his stride. How? By keeping your emotions in check. Why? Because it's what he is *not* used to seeing.

In the beginning, all it takes is a **hint of indifference**. If a man can't tell where you're coming from (completely) and doesn't have assurances of what you want, he respects you more and treats you better. This hooks him because he doesn't have the "pull" he's used to having.

Here's how. You have to be able to sit next to a man while hugging and kissing . . . and at the same you have to *keep yourself emotionally ten feet away*. Even if you are sitting *in* his lap, your heart has to stay locked in the trunk of your car—next to the spare tire. You can be warm and affectionate. But stop telling yourself "He is the one!" And stop rationalizing, "He is different. He makes me feel something I haven't felt in years." Instead, you have to think: "I'm willing to learn more. I'm enjoying myself, but if it doesn't work out, there are other ducks on the pond."

Most women start off on "tilt" because they show they care *too* much *too* soon. Soon after, she's freefalling (by herself) after which he makes the following observation: "She is not in control of her emotions." Or as one man named Connor explained, "When I meet a woman and take her out a few times, I'm wondering, 'Who is in control? Her . . . or her emotions?'" If it's your emotions, you will be at his mercy. It's a guy thing. They learn very early that showing too much emotion is the same as showing weakness. They respect women who are strong. So you have to keep watch on how much emotion you show.

Therefore:

FORMULA FOR FAILURE:
No Emotional Control = Desperation to Keep Him = A Free Ride for Him

FORMULA FOR SUCCESS:
Emotional Self-Control = Control over How You Are Treated and Control over Whether You Are Respected

Men think that if you are deeply attached right away and no longer in charge of yourself emotionally, you will *tolerate almost anything* (only to cry about it later). And you'll even make excuses. "He really is busy with work" or "He just got out of a relationship." A man is more inclined to treat a woman like a sex toy or trophy when she lacks emotional self-control and buys the B.S. That's when he rides the horsey . . . without putting a quarter in the meter.

In other words, he'll continue to see her, but whenever it's convenient for him. When a woman becomes too attached too soon *because of her emotions* . . . or shows signs she's not in control after sex *because of her emotions* . . . or expects a fairy-tale happy ending *because of her emotions* . . . she is putting herself on the dinner table.

Conversely: When she is less tolerant and has her wits about her, she'll call him out when he attempts to "condition" her to receive less. The first time he tries to come over late at night, he gets intercepted at the door. "Don't call me five minutes before you want to see me. Although I am deeply touched that you decided to shove me into your busy schedule, please give me a bit more notice next time." Then her stock goes up.

Men size women up and feel them out. He wants to know if you live in a fairy tale and want to grow up to be a "princess"—or whether you are independent and level-headed, with goals of your own. If they cannot tell where you're coming from and don't always know what you will do next, they respect you more and treat you better. And that opens up avenues for him to become attached and fall for you.

A side-by-side comparison:

EMOTIONAL INTENSITY . . .	vs.	A HINT OF INDIFFERENCE . . .
If he senses you are 100% hooked within the first month . . .		If he senses you're curious and willing to learn more, and you aren't following the pattern that most women follow . . .
. . . he will think he has complete control. That makes him lose interest and see you less often.		. . . he thinks: "Gee, I wonder why she's not buying into it?"
. . . then he'll begin to see what he can get away with. If behaves in a less-than-gentlemanly way, he assumes you'll forgive him.		. . . then he'll begin to see you as an individual and a real person—not just a hump toy. He'll begin to see, "There is a lot more here." That keeps his interest.

The most important thing is to break the pattern of what he's used to seeing. When a man sees you keep your distance ever-so-slightly, and you are outside his reach—and that you don't give him a "free pass"—that hooks him and keeps him interested. He gets hooked when he doesn't have the mental "pull" he's used to having because he has not yet won. That's when it becomes a mental challenge. "I have to be a better man to get and keep this one." That's how you get a proper courtship.

Some women try to communicate their strategy, and approach these issues verbally. The next letter illustrates this.

Dear Sherry,

I have my own career and my own life. Men see this. And I tell them I will not tolerate bullshit of any kind. And I express that I want to be able to be who I am. I want to be able to show what makes me happy and sad. I want to be able to talk about everything and anything. Wouldn't the right guy want me to be myself? I am a strong woman. But men often seem intimidated by me.

—Anonymous Nice Girl

Men are not afraid of strong women. A man named Michael explained, "Men are not afraid of strong women, they are afraid of a woman with very strong jaw muscles and overly-active vocal cords." Then he told a story:

"A lot of women don't realize that their own worst enemy is their mouth. If she whines and complains a lot, it doesn't matter if she's the most beautiful woman in the world.

(Translation? No emotional control.) I remember a blind date where I picked up a woman and started driving to meet two other couples at a restaurant forty minutes away. The whole way to the restaurant my date kept saying, 'I'm hungry. I'm starved. I'm hungry. I'm starved. How much longer is it going to be?' She knew where the restaurant was, and how long it would take to get there. But she nagged the whole way and didn't stop venting her discomfort. I decided before we got to the restaurant that I'd never take her out again."

The less you telegraph or dictate verbally, the better. The more you talk, the less you can read what he's doing and where he's coming from. To a man, the worst kind of partner is the one to whom—no matter what he gives—it will never be good enough.

You get a lot further by "flying below radar" and playing up your feminine side. Your feminine side disarms men because they have no defense to it. Men are not afraid of strong women . . . they are put off by women who have *lost their femininity*. Dolly Parton, who is one of the most successful businesswomen and well-respected songwriters in Nashville, said something interesting in a *60 Minutes* interview recently. She said: "A lot of men thought I was as silly as I looked. I look like a woman but I think like a man. And in this world of business, that has helped me a lot. Because by the time they think that I don't know what's going on . . . I done got the money, and gone." Her femininity keeps her stealth. She stays ahead of the game by flying below radar.

As a general rule, don't telegraph or announce what you want. Not only do you communicate your strategy, you also reduce the mystery in the relationship. If you don't like what you see, raise the issue when it comes up. If his response is not acceptable, then leave. But don't telegraph to a guy *up front* (who you barely know) what makes you happy or what makes you upset. If you do, many men will use the information to manipulate you. He'll do what you like just long enough to get what he wants. Or, he'll do it to get forgiveness for something he's done wrong.

This is how that plays out. . . .

Dear Sherry,

I've been dating a guy on and off. It seems like a vicious cycle. We have been on this insane merry-go-ride for two years. We are very passionate in bed, but outside the bed he is emotionally unavailable and the relationship is not progressing. I have left him a million times only for him to chase me with e-mails, phone calls, and showing up at my home or work. He tells me "this time will be different" and he is "going to change." He begs me not to leave him and tells me he needs me. I take him back and he is good for a day or two then goes back to his selfish ways. I do love him but this emotional merry-go-round is making me dizzy.

—Anonymous Nice Girl

If there are any men reading this scenario, they are green with envy. "Man, all that great sex . . . for free?"

If a relationship is on-and-off within the first year, that's an immediate sign you are wasting your time. He's not "hot and cold" because he's indecisive. He's "hot and cold" because he is manipulating you. Let's define:

> ## THE "HOT-AND-COLD" RELATIONSHIP
> **When he's "hot," he is *manipulating* you.**
> **When he's "cold," he is showing his *true* colors.**

If you think, "If only we can reconnect and sleep together. Then it will escalate into a relationship," you are helping him manipulate you. When a guy you've known a while calls once a week, you can't think, "Yay! My plan is finally working." Because what he's saying to himself is, "Cool, this one I can sleep with every two weeks," and then he tries to find another woman he can sleep with in between. What I often hear from women is: "But I really want this guy. We had great chemistry. How can I spike his interest?" They are just not willing to accept that "this guy" is manipulating them, or that *that is who he is.*

The question I often hear from women is, "How do I stop thinking about him? How do I stop caring so much?" If you are on a diet, you can't think about chocolate cake constantly, right? Same goes for relationships. Many women are so gripped with fear over the loss of a man that they think of him constantly. Stopping that unhealthy obsession solves 90 percent of the problem, and lifts all the pain. When you are no longer obsessed, men sense it. You often get what you want. This gives the power back to you.

If you want to control your emotions, you have to control your thoughts. As Eleanor Roosevelt said, "You must do the thing you think you cannot do." The best chance at success with a particular guy is when you are not intensely attached. Whether you are starting a relationship and you want to keep your feet on the ground, or you are ending one and need to detach, the following exercise will help. The key is to stop thinking about him altogether—cold turkey.

How to Stop Thinking about Him

- Whenever you think about him, STOP.
- Consciously replace the thought of him with another thought or activity.
- It must be a feel-good thought or activity.
- The key is to distract yourself, immediately.
- Do this repeatedly, each time he pops into your head.
- Get creative. Immediately turn on your favorite show, eat your favorite meal, go to the gym, or get out for a walk.
- Each and every time you think of him—without exception —stop the worry and pain and force yourself to experience the opposite. Do something that *feels good*.

If you are at work, get your favorite coffee. If you are in the car, put in a feel-good CD. When children cry, you distract them with a toy, right? You have to break the downward spiral of negativity and force yourself to focus on positive things that have *nothing to do with him*. If you do this ten times a day for a few days, you will break the habit of obsessing over him. That is how you lift the pain and pull yourself back up by your own bootstraps.

In *Paradise Lost*, John Milton wrote, "The mind is its own place, and in itself can make a heaven of hell, a hell of heaven." In Chapter 2 we talked about not seeing a new guy all the time or for too many consecutive nights in a row. And readers follow this advice. Where they screw up is that while they are not in his company, they think about the guy constantly—and form an unhealthy dependence. You may as well move in with him the first week if you are going to think of him twenty-four hours a day.

While you detach, always re-evaluate your "prize." If he still isn't giving you what you want, the question to ask yourself is whether you really want him. Maybe he's a bratty child in an adult body and never went through the rites of passage from "boy" to "man" . . . and his mamma still does his laundry which gives him a false sense of grandiosity. When you encounter a guy like that, don't assume you are no longer desirable. You have to get up, dust yourself off, and say, "He isn't the person I thought he was. I need to dust myself off and invest my energy elsewhere." As Maya Angelou said, "When people show you who they are, believe them . . . the *first* time."

With a good man, he's not thinking, "How can I take?" He's thinking, "How can I give?" A quality man wants to keep his wife or girlfriend happy—emotionally. It's ego: "I am *man enough* to please my woman!" That makes him feel like a stud. Now let's define happy: Happiness is not getting scraps.

Don't take it personally. Very little has anything to do with you. Many people lack the basic equipment to be in a relationship and there's nothing you can do to change it. You can't take a skunk and dip it in perfume and hope it becomes a puppy. Eventually, the perfume will wear off and you'll still have a skunk on your hands.

Always look at who you are dealing with; what you see is what you get. His character won't change. His career might change, his clothing might change, his priorities might change, his residence might change. But his character will stay the same.

The men who think it's okay to give scraps to you lack this basic equipment necessary for a good relationship.

WHAT IS THE BASIC EMOTIONAL EQUIPMENT?

- **Character and decency**
- **A stand-up person**
- **Consideration for others**
- **Appreciation for kindness**
- **A sense of proportion with respect to how much a person gives, and how much they take**
- **Loyalty to those who are loyal to you**

I remember that a teacher of mine once said, "Make those people important . . . those people who make *you* important." It's not that hard, if everyone makes an effort. And if it's become hard, and you feel like a slave laborer in this relationship, stop punishing yourself. Misery is not a return. You have full control over how you are made to feel. You may feel like you are handcuffed and bound—but you are holding the key to those cuffs and can very easily take them off.

If you are seeing a guy for several months, and you allow him to see you once a week—for sex—and on top of that you are wanting more from the relationship, you are signaling to him that he can take advantage of you. Sex is not something you do to reward someone or to score a relationship. Sex is something you do with a man who already cares about you. If months have gone by and you aren't talking at least every other day, that's not a relationship. This is often when the nice girl instinct kicks into overdrive. Here's the succession of logic:

> *"He was wonderful in the beginning."*
> *"I must have screwed things up."*
> *"I need to . . . do more . . . work harder . . . jump higher . . ."*
> *". . . and pick up a two-by-four and beat myself up with it by*
>   *wearing myself out and telling myself I'm not worthy."*

Life is hard enough; you don't need anyone around darkening your doorstep to make it worse. It's not always you. Maybe it's just not a good fit. Maybe he just doesn't have the basic equipment (and nor will he with *any* woman).

So remember, have a wait-and-see attitude and, while you learn about him, keep a parachute on your heart. With a good guy, if you regulate or slow down what you give early on, you will see what kind of person you are dealing with. The cream will rise to the top. When you give a little and then wait to see what comes back, the guy who is worth having around will give also. If he cools off, a hint of indifference acts as a trigger. He will be concerned about what you are feeling. A woman can tell how much a man cares by how much he remembers what she likes, and whether he's doing things to make her happy.

That's the big picture: your happiness. And health. You should never care what a man thinks of you—*until he demonstrates to you that he cares about making you happy*. If he isn't trying to make you happy, then send him back from "whence" he came because winning him over will have no benefit. At the end of the day, happiness, joy, . . . and yes . . . your "emotional stability" . . . those comprise the only measuring stick you really need to have.

11

THE

New AND *Improved*

BITCH

The Survival Guide for Women Who Are Too Nice

"Always give them the old fire. Even when you feel like a squashed cake of ice."
—ETHEL MERMAN

The Bitch Stands Her Ground

The "new and improved" bitch is not a bad thing. She is a refined version of the proverbial, "old" bitch. She's not abrasive or mean, nor does she nag to get what she wants. She speaks with her actions, and she's only a bitch when she *has to be*. One of the most telling signs that a woman "has arrived" is that she's not obsessed with pleasing a man, or anyone other than herself. Who is this "new and improved bitch?" See the following definition:

> **Bitch** (noun): A woman who won't bang her head against the wall obsessing over someone else's opinion—be it a man or anyone else in her life. She understands that if someone does not approve of her, it's just one person's opinion; therefore, it's of no real importance. She doesn't try to live up to anyone else's standards—only her own. Because of this, she relates to a man very differently.

The bitch also perceives *herself* differently. She'll get into the "boxing ring," so to speak, with the mindset that she's an "equal opponent" to a man. With a nice girl, a man automatically thinks of himself as the "heavyweight" and of her as the "featherweight" (a.k.a., the underdog). A confident woman who enters the ring and doesn't go down without a fight earns the respect of a man, even if she loses. Why? Because then he knows she's a woman with *heart*. If she goes down, she goes down swinging. And when they step out of the ring, he can't help but have more respect for her.

The bitch behaves in a way that a man understands. She speaks to him in the same language he uses when he talks to his male friends, which, again, lets him know she's on a level playing field. She is able to communicate without a lot of "gray area," and she's forthright. Don't think this matters? Take a peek at a side-by-side comparison:

THE NICE GIRL	THE BITCH
She'll try to sweet-talk a man into giving her what she wants on a regular basis. If she doesn't get it, she'll cry, get upset, or pout.	She won't sugarcoat anything or use euphemisms. She is direct about what her preferences are and lets him know what the dos and don'ts are, with respect to how he treats her.
She'll play the guilt card or talk about her "inner child"; she seems to possess a childlike quality.	She is a grown woman, so there's nothing "childlike" about her. She has a no-nonsense philosophy.
If he hurts her in some way, she'll cry. Then she'll make him apologize and promise not to do it again.	She'll back off and let her silence do the talking. Then she'll communicate when she's ready, on her own terms; at this point, she makes it clear it won't happen again, because if it does she won't be around.
She tells herself, "He didn't mean that." Or, she makes excuses if he behaves badly.	She notices his disrespect instantly and, without hesitation, calls him on the carpet over it.

(continued)

THE NICE GIRL	THE BITCH
She forces herself to do something she is uncomfortable with in order to please a man. She also puts on a happy face and pretends that she likes it.	She won't do anything she's not comfortable with and won't hesitate to let him know. She meets him on a level playing field.
ONE = A DOCILE WOMAN = LOSS OF RESPECT	**THE OTHER = A DESIRABLE WOMAN = INCREASED RESPECT**

Rarely, if ever, will two grown men have a drawn-out conversation that ends with: "You hurt my feelings!" The closest thing a man will say to another man about feelings is, "You really pissed me off."

As an example, hypothetically, one guy may borrow money from his friend and not pay it back. A long mushy conversation will not take place. If any exchange happens at all, it's short and sweet and ends with, "Screw you, asshole!" Then they stop hanging out together and that's the end of it.

Because the bitch will "tell it like it is," a man will respect the way she communicates. In a man's eyes, anger isn't weakness. He'll think she has more *self-control* than a woman who is emotional. With the emotional woman, he'll rationalize that she's hormonally unbalanced because of her monthly cycle. Or he'll think she's weak. But, with a bitch, he'll think she knows what she does and doesn't want. She knows what she likes and what she dislikes. She has "spirit." (And I don't mean the cheerleading kind.)

When you say the word *B-I-T-C-H* out loud, don't say it like it's a *bad* thing. According to some, the word derives from the first letters in the following phrase: **B**abe **I**n **T**otal

Control of **H**erself. The only higher crown, the only higher *honor*, is to be called a "High-Maintenance Bitch." It's a sign of success, indicating that this is the woman the guy *ends up keeping*. If nothing else, he keeps her for the very practical reason that he's invested so much that he can't let her go. And he's *still* trying to win her over.

ATTRACTION PRINCIPLE #95
**A man feels he's won, or conquered a woman,
when she eats out of the palm of his hand.
At which point, he begins to get bored.**

The Bitch Is Never Fully Conquered

So why do men love bitches? With a bitch, they never feel as though they've quite conquered her, so they keep trying. Some men try for a lifetime.

When a man is with a woman who is willing to bend over backward, it almost invites mistreatment. Charlotte catered to her boyfriend, Tom, *constantly*. His interest was starting to fade.

Charlotte thought she'd win Tom back by throwing a party for him on the beach. She planned an elaborate party and invited all his friends. She also decided to pay over $3,000 to hire a sky-writing service for the event. There were two planes and they made a big beautiful heart in the sky followed by the words, "I love you always." Once the planes arrived overhead, it took almost a half-hour for them to do an exquisite job. When they were finished, everyone was in awe. It was breathtaking, and everyone thought so—*except* Tom (who had unfortunately called an hour previously to say he couldn't make it). By then, it was too late for Charlotte to get a refund on the fortune she had spent. She tried to cancel, but it was too late. The planes had already taken off and were en route to the party.

The example with Charlotte is not uncommon. This is what happens when a woman is *too nice* and will jump through hoops: *It invites bad behavior.*

While the nice girl loses her mind, the bitch, on the other hand, makes the man lose his. When a woman keeps a level head, a man will often become much more intrigued with her. He'll think about her constantly, he won't be able to get enough of her, and he'll eventually decide he can't live without her.

It's a basic difference between men and women: Women want safety and predictability and men long for excitement, danger, and unpredictability. As a child, the nice girl played with Barbie and her Ken doll; she grew up with the mental image that she, too, would live "happily ever after." Little boys want nothing to do with the Ken doll—they identify with *exciting* figures who live dangerously, like Batman, Superman, and Spiderman.

Ask any mother which child she finds more troublesome—a son or a daughter. Most mothers confess that boys are more difficult, especially if there are more tha n one. Why? For most men, safe = boring. So they look for ways to add excitement and danger, and go out of their way to pursue things that are difficult. It's this very *element of danger* that draws him to a bitch.

ATTRACTION PRINCIPLE #96
The *tension* that arises with a slightly bitchy woman gives a subtle feeling of danger to a man. He feels slightly unsure because she is never in the palm of his hand.

Think about what things men collect, or the things that fascinate them. Guns, ammunition, sports cards, sci-fi magazines, pocket knives, little metal cars, power tools, and a "rechargeable" flashlight. (Your job is to act riveted. "Wow, rechargeable?") Oh, and let's not forget the "priceless" collection of little army men (just to die for) and the high-speed stuff: cars, Jet Skis, motorcycles, and airplanes.

The nice girl makes the mistake of nurturing a man and making him feel too "safe." Men get bored very easily, which is why too much predictability and safety makes the relationship seem *monotonous* to him. With the bitch, it isn't monotonous.

The nice girl buries her head in the sand when she ignores a man's need for stimulation, danger, or "a challenge." This is to her detriment. She's like an ostrich. When an ostrich sees a hunting animal, instead of facing the tiger head-on, it'll bury its head in the sand. Hence, it becomes "din din."

The bitch takes the head-on approach, but the nice girl takes the "buried head" approach. The bitch sees what's actually there. *The nice girl sees what she wants to see.*

In the first month alone, here's what the "nice girl" will do . . . She'll give him a foot massage. Then she'll cook eggs with six ingredients and pancakes on the side. She'll drive to do his laundry and iron his shirts. Then she'll read him poems and want to cuddle all day. After he dumps her, she'll say, "I can't believe he did this to me!"

Many women believe that men want a woman who will do . . . *whatever* they tell her to do. In theory, men want this. But in practice, when they actually get it, *they'll tire of it almost instantaneously*.

The minute a man thinks he can "do no wrong" in your eyes and you'll accept anything he dishes out, you've already "waved a white flag" with regard to his having the hots for you. His desire will come to a screeching halt.

Don't buy the one about him wanting a "damsel in distress," either. As one man said, "When you rescue a damsel in distress, all you get stuck with is a distressed damsel."

The notion that a woman has to "spill her guts out" in order to truly be in love isn't a sign of love, it's about becoming "din din." He sees a docile woman and he says to himself, "Oh, no. A cling-on. Am I going to have to carry around this bag of Jell-O forever?" Once he realizes this, he calls less often or stops calling altogether—*after* he has sex with her.

ATTRACTION PRINCIPLE #97
**A "yes" woman who gives *too* much sends the impression that she believes in the man more than she believes in herself.
Men view this as *weakness* not *kindness*.**

When the nice girl needs a man too much and puts him on a pedestal, she treats him with a view of himself that *even he* doesn't hold. And it makes him very uncomfortable because he knows (better than anyone) that he "ain't no white knight." But he knows it's her fantasy, so he gives it the "good ol' college try." He makes a forced effort to try to be romantic, and it isn't long before he begins to question whether she's being disingenuous, too. He thinks to himself, "*Hmm . . . I* wonder what she's really like. She can't possibly be *that* nice." Like a low-interest-rate credit card that's only good for the first month, he'll start to feel he's getting the "promo package." Not the real deal.

With the bitch, it's straight-up and real. There's no concern that either side will do a "bait and switch." He tests her once or twice, and she puts him in his place each time. Then two things happen. First, he says to himself, "This one's not dumb. She won't buy my bullcrap."

Second, he feels as though she's seen him for who he really is. She's seen "the worst," and she likes him anyway. Likewise, he's seen "the worst" in her, so he doesn't feel as though there is a surprise "lurking" inside her. When he's with a bitch, he may be annoyed from time to time, but he believes that what they share is *real*.

The Bitch Is Defined from Within

Eddie Murphy once said in an interview: "The best advice I ever heard is, don't take anyone else's advice." There's power in this because it puts you in the conductor's seat, right at "the controls" in your life. It doesn't mean you should stop seeking information or outside input, it just means that you're the one driving. You choose your own destination.

This attitude directly impacts whether a man will view you as independent. The minute you stop being an independent thinker and he starts having to think for you, you catapult right out of the "driver's" seat and land right in the "doormat" seat. *The minute someone else can dictate what you think or how you feel about yourself, you are at their mercy.*

This attitude also influences success in many other areas. As long as you let someone else make decisions regarding your career, dreams, or aspirations, you've limited yourself drastically. *You'll only be as good as that person allows you to become.*

ATTRACTION PRINCIPLE #98
**Be an independent thinker at all times,
and ignore anyone who attempts to define
you in a limiting way.**

Whether it's your taste in clothing, your needs in a relationship, or what you do for a living—don't let anyone else be at the controls. Define yourself.

The minute you become an independent thinker, two things will happen. First, positive people and things will be drawn to you like a magnet. Second, it will serve as a deterrent for negative people who will try to distract you from achieving your goals. There will always be people who will be there to plant negative seeds in your garden, *if you make yourself available for that.*

Standing up for yourself doesn't always involve verbal confrontation. Sometimes it's about not wasting energy on people who are negative.

ATTRACTION PRINCIPLE #99
Truly powerful people don't explain why they want respect. They simply don't engage someone who doesn't give it to them.

This may seem very simple and obvious to a person with self-esteem, but it's usually the very thing that the nice girl does *not* do. She'll cosign on the dotted line for a guy who has lousy credit. She'll sleep with him before knowing his middle name. And above all, she'll let him decide what her value is as a woman, instead of deciding this for herself.

Kindness is always the first choice. But there are times when you can't be kind to someone who doesn't have your best interests in mind. When you see this behavior, it's appropriate to be kind to *yourself* by responding to it, either by correcting the situation or by not allowing the person to have access to you.

The bitch can be a soft—and very feminine—woman, but she still has a quiet dignity. This woman lets people know in a graceful way that she won't be easily manipulated. She won't jump through hoops. And she won't define herself by what other people think.

A perfect example is my soft-spoken Japanese friend Masae. She's been living in the United States for less than a year, and she speaks broken English with a Japanese accent. Nevertheless, she's a wonderful example of the grace and quiet strength that I'm describing.

Masae was seeing an American man named Steven for some time. It was his birthday, so she decided to cook him a Japanese feast. She made miso soup, several types of sushi, and two authentic hot main courses. She was also an exemplary hostess. The only feedback Steven gave was that the soy sauce was too salty. "Next time get the one with the green lid, because it's lower in sodium."

Masae was astonished, but she kept her composure. She said to him, with her limited language skills, "I cook for you. But if you complain? I no do for you." She's had nothing but praise ever since.

As Eleanor Roosevelt said, "No one can make you feel inferior without your consent." A positive person will say *positive* things, especially when you aren't feeling up. When you leave his company, you'll feel as though your batteries have been recharged. When you meet someone who is truly great, he makes you believe you can be great, too. This is the kind of relationship you want, and it's the only kind of relationship worth having.

The longer you practice being an independent thinker, the more attractive you'll be. You'll put a "magic spell" on a man. A deadly "mojo." You'll wake up and feel happier than you've ever been. Your aura and your life force will slowly come back.

The media doesn't perpetuate this; instead they fuel a "cookie cutter" mentality that women are supposed to fit into a box. "Wear this because this is hot." (Change the channel.) "You have got to get this look." (Change the channel.) "Say those affirmation jingles: Claim it; then shame it. Own it and condone it . . ." (Change the channel.) "This organic hair color will turn heads."

When a woman is secure with herself, she isn't afraid to define herself and defy public opinion. She has her own look. Her own style. Her own charisma. Her own brand of charm. A man wants something he doesn't see every day. Not in terms of a redhead versus a blonde. He wants the rare woman *who can think for herself.*

When it comes to a commitment or a relationship with most women, many men feel like lion trainers. It's as though they have to use a chair to get the lions to back away. "Back off . . . back off . . ." So when they meet a woman who has the confidence to hold her own—or make them come her way—it has a different effect. They're not used to it, so they become intrigued.

The bitch isn't afraid to be different, which is why she won't be a "booty call" or a pearl on a long string of pearls. She won't be a man's late-night convenience. She won't be doing lap dances. She won't be afraid to turn thirty or forty years old. At any age, this woman will feel like a "prize." She won't be defined by the media's perception of aging; she won't be made to feel like defective livestock because she is no longer a teenager. Married, single, or divorced, this woman feels good about herself.

A woman with an exterior that is too tough is not the "new and improved" bitch I'm speaking of. Abrasiveness is *not* the objective. In Italy, there is a very common expression: *È tutto fumo e niente arrosto.* Literally, it means, "There is plenty of smoke, but nothing is getting roasted." When a woman is too abrasive or too bitchy, or she pretends to be too much of anything, she rarely has anything to back it up. The "new and improved bitch" is truly strong, because she is nice. But she also demands the same kindness in return.

The Bitch Has a Strong Will and Faith in Herself

When I set out to talk to men about this book, I wasn't sure what to expect. I thought that some might react to the title, *Why Men Love Bitches*, and say, "Men don't love bitches!" What happened was the exact opposite. They absolutely confirmed—over and over—that a strong woman is very much a turn-on. Sometimes they described why they love bitches. Other times they asked, " Yeah, why do we love bitches?" But over 90 percent of the time, they didn't deny the fact that they're turned on by strong women.

Putting yourself first is not something men resent. On the contrary, a man actually respects it. He feels as though there is far less weight on his shoulders when you are independent, and he doesn't have to make you happy all the time. He'll regard you as a secure woman, instead of as a ditsy or flighty woman who doesn't know what she wants.

Putting yourself first means going back and relearning how to count. In math, the number one comes before the number two (1 . . . 2 . . . again . . . 1 . . . 2 . . .). You are number one and—are you sitting down?—*he is number two!* Until now, you've made the mistake of starting to count at "number two." Number one wasn't even counted. You skipped over *numero uno* because you didn't seem to feel you mattered.

Life is an extension of grade school. A third grader approaches another kid and bullies him. He slaps the kid, steals his lunch money, and runs. The child who won't be bullied is the child who slaps the bully and takes his lunch money back. (With an extra little slap, just for thinking he could have gotten away with it.)

The *new and improved bitch* understands this principle in adult day-to-day life. People will do the same thing on a daily basis. They'll try to slap you and run, whether it's a coworker, a family member, a friend, or yes . . . even a lover. The only difference is none of these people will try to steal your lunch money. Instead, consciously or not, they'll steal your self-confidence.

When it comes to believing in yourself, put your eye on the mark and don't blink. If you have a goal, a dream, or an aspiration . . . believe in yourself while you are *on the way* to your destination, and you will have already arrived.

Throughout life, people will try to shake your faith *in yourself*. When this happens, remind yourself that the only way they can succeed is if you allow it. When you walk down the street of life, always hold your head high and keep walking. Don't *ever* let anyone shake your faith in yourself, because that's really *all* that you have.

ATTRACTION PRINCIPLE #100
The most attractive quality of all is dignity.

Appendix

SHERRY'S *Attraction* PRINCIPLES

ATTRACTION PRINCIPLE #1
Anything a person chases in life runs away.

ATTRACTION PRINCIPLE #2
**The women who have the men climbing the walls for
them aren't always exceptional. Often, they are the
ones who don't appear to care that much.**

ATTRACTION PRINCIPLE #3
**A woman is perceived as offering a mental challenge
to the degree that a man doesn't feel
he has a 100 percent hold on her.**

ATTRACTION PRINCIPLE #4
**Sometimes a man deliberately won't call,
just to see how you'll respond.**

ATTRACTION PRINCIPLE #5
**If you start out dependent, it turns him off.
But if it is something he can't have, it becomes more
of a challenge for him to get it.**

ATTRACTION PRINCIPLE #6
**It is your attitude about yourself
that a man will adopt.**

ATTRACTION PRINCIPLE #7
Act like a prize and you'll turn him into a believer.

ATTRACTION PRINCIPLE #8
**The biggest variable between a bitch
and a woman who is too nice is *fear*.
The bitch shows that she's
not afraid to be without him.**

ATTRACTION PRINCIPLE #9
**If the choice is between her dignity
and having a relationship, the bitch will
prioritize her dignity above all else.**

ATTRACTION PRINCIPLE #10
**When a woman doesn't give in easily and doesn't
appear docile or submissive, it becomes more
stimulating to obtain her.**

ATTRACTION PRINCIPLE #11
**Being right on the verge of getting something
generates a desire that has to be satisfied.**

ATTRACTION PRINCIPLE #12
**A man knows which woman will give in to
last-minute requests.**

ATTRACTION PRINCIPLE #13
Whether you have terms and conditions indicates whether you have options. Almost immediately, you present yourself as a doormat or a dreamgirl.

ATTRACTION PRINCIPLE #14
If you smother him, he'll go into defense mode and look for an escape route to protect his freedom.

ATTRACTION PRINCIPLE #15
Whenever a woman requires too many things from a man, he'll resent it. Let him give what he wants to give freely; then observe who he is.

ATTRACTION PRINCIPLE #16
A bitch gives a man plenty of space so he doesn't fear being trapped in a cage. Then . . . he sets out to trap her in his.

ATTRACTION PRINCIPLE #17
If you tell him you are not interested in jumping into a relationship with both feet, he will set out to try to change your mind.

ATTRACTION PRINCIPLE #18
Always give the appearance that he has plenty of space. It gets him to drop his guard.

ATTRACTION PRINCIPLE #19
More than anything else, he watches to see if you'll be too emotionally dependent on him.

ATTRACTION PRINCIPLE #20
He must feel that you choose to be with him, not that you need to be with him. Only then will he perceive you as an equal partner.

ATTRACTION PRINCIPLE #21
If a man has to wait before he sleeps with a woman, he'll not only perceive her as more beautiful, he'll also take time to appreciate who she is.

ATTRACTION PRINCIPLE #22
Sex and the "spark" are not one and the same.

ATTRACTION PRINCIPLE #23
Before sex, a man isn't thinking clearly and a woman is thinking clearly. After sex, it reverses. The man is thinking clearly and the woman isn't.

ATTRACTION PRINCIPLE #24
Every man wants to have sex *first*; whether he wants a girlfriend is something he thinks about *later*. By not giving him what he wants up front, you become his girlfriend without him realizing it.

ATTRACTION PRINCIPLE #25
A man intuitively senses whether sexuality comes from a place of security or from a place of neediness. He knows when a woman is having sex to appease him.

ATTRACTION PRINCIPLE #26
Bad habits are easier to form than good ones, because good habits require conscious effort. Waiting encourages this effort.

ATTRACTION PRINCIPLE #27
If you pull the sexual plug at the last minute, he'll label you a tease.

ATTRACTION PRINCIPLE #28
If he makes you feel insecure, let your insecurity be your guide.

ATTRACTION PRINCIPLE #29
**A quality guy fantasizes about a woman
who genuinely loves sex.**

ATTRACTION PRINCIPLE #30
**Any time a woman competes with
another woman, she demeans herself.**

ATTRACTION PRINCIPLE #31
**When there is that undeniable "spark,"
there is only one key to the lock.**

ATTRACTION PRINCIPLE #32
**Let him think he's in control. He'll automatically
start doing things you want done because he'll
always want to look like "a king" in your eyes.**

ATTRACTION PRINCIPLE #33
**When you cater to his ego in a soft way, he doesn't try
to get power in an aggressive way.**

ATTRACTION PRINCIPLE #34
**When you appear softer and more feminine,
you appeal to his instinct to *protect*.
When you appear more aggressive, you
appeal to his instinct to *compete*.**

ATTRACTION PRINCIPLE #35
He'll let a woman who becomes his doormat
pay for dinner on the first couple of dates,
but he wouldn't *think* of it with his *dreamgirl*.

ATTRACTION PRINCIPLE #36
The token power position is for public display, but
the true power position is for private viewing only.
And this is the only one that matters.

ATTRACTION PRINCIPLE #37
If you give him a feeling of power, he'll want to
protect you and he'll want to give you the world.

ATTRACTION PRINCIPLE #38
When a woman acts as though she's capable of
everything, she gets stuck doing everything.

ATTRACTION PRINCIPLE #39
Men don't respond to words.
They respond to no contact.

ATTRACTION PRINCIPLE #40
Talking about the "relationship" too much
takes away the element of the "unknown"
and thus the mystery.

ATTRACTION PRINCIPLE #41
**Men respect women who communicate
in a succinct way, because it's the language
men use to talk to one another.**

ATTRACTION PRINCIPLE #42
When you are always HAPPY;

And he is always free to GO;

He feels LUCKY.

ATTRACTION PRINCIPLE #43
**If you allow your rhythm to be interrupted,
you'll create a void. Then, to replace what
you give up, you'll start to expect and
need more from your partner.**

ATTRACTION PRINCIPLE #44
**Most women are starving to receive something from a
man that they need to give to themselves.**

ATTRACTION PRINCIPLE #45
**A woman looks more secure in a man's eyes
when he can't pull her away from her life,
because she is *content* with her life.**

ATTRACTION PRINCIPLE #46
The second a woman works overtime to make herself fit his criteria, she has lowered the standard of that relationship.

ATTRACTION PRINCIPLE #47
You jump through hoops any time you repeatedly make it very obvious you're giving your "all."

ATTRACTION PRINCIPLE #48
You have to keep from being sucked down into quicksand. Unless you maintain control over yourself, the relationship is doomed.

ATTRACTION PRINCIPLE #49
Jumping through hoops often has a negative outcome: He sees it as an opportunity to have his cake and eat it, too. But when you stay just outside his reach, he'll stay on his best behavior.

ATTRACTION PRINCIPLE #50
The nice girl gives away too much of herself when pleasing him regularly becomes more important than pleasing herself.

ATTRACTION PRINCIPLE #51
**The relationship may not be right for you
if you find yourself jumping through hoops.
When something is right, it will feel
easier and much more effortless.**

ATTRACTION PRINCIPLE #52
**When you nag, he tunes you out.
But when you speak with your actions,
he pays attention.**

ATTRACTION PRINCIPLE #53
**When a man takes a woman for granted, he still looks
for reassurance that she is still "right there."**

ATTRACTION PRINCIPLE #54
**When the routine becomes predictable, he's more
likely to give you the same type of love he had
for his mother—and the odds that he will
take you for granted increase.**

ATTRACTION PRINCIPLE #55
**Negative attention is still attention.
It lets a man know that he has you—
right where he wants you.**

ATTRACTION PRINCIPLE #56
When you treat him casually as though he's a friend, he'll come your way. Because he wants things to be romantic, but he also *wants* to be the pursuer.

ATTRACTION PRINCIPLE #57
A little distance combined with the appearance of self-control makes him nervous that he may be losing you.

ATTRACTION PRINCIPLE #58
A man takes a woman for granted when he's interested, but will no longer go out of his way.

ATTRACTION PRINCIPLE #59
When you nag, *you* become the problem, and he deals with it by tuning you out. But when you don't nag, he deals with *the problem*.

ATTRACTION PRINCIPLE #60
If you take his chores away from him and praise someone else for doing it, he'll want his chores back.

ATTRACTION PRINCIPLE #61
When you nag, he sees weakness.

ATTRACTION PRINCIPLE #62
**He perceives an emotional woman
as more of a pushover.**

ATTRACTION PRINCIPLE #63
**In the same way that familiarity breeds contempt, a
slightly aloof demeanor can often renew his respect.**

ATTRACTION PRINCIPLE #64
**He'll forget what he has in you . . .
unless you remind him.**

ATTRACTION PRINCIPLE #65
**Many women talk a lot out of nervousness—
which is something that men will often
perceive as insecurity.**

ATTRACTION PRINCIPLE #66
**Talking about feelings to a man will
feel like *work*. When he's with a woman,
he wants it to feel like *fun*.**

ATTRACTION PRINCIPLE #67
**Forcing him to talk about feelings all the
time will not only make you seem needy,
it will eventually make him lose respect.
And when he loses respect, he'll pay
even less attention to your feelings.**

ATTRACTION PRINCIPLE #68
**In the beginning, the only thing you need
to pay attention to is whether he keeps coming
around, because he'll only be able to suspend or hide
his emotions for so long.**

ATTRACTION PRINCIPLE #69
**Men treat women the way they treat other men. They
"play it cool" because they don't want to appear weak
or desperate.**

ATTRACTION PRINCIPLE #70
**The element of surprise both inside and
outside of the bedroom is important to men,
and it adds to the excitement.**

ATTRACTION PRINCIPLE #71
**Don't always do the same thing over and over
in the bedroom. Vary it so that it doesn't
become a predictable routine.**

ATTRACTION PRINCIPLE #72
Most men tend to disrespect a woman who appears to be too *malleable*.

ATTRACTION PRINCIPLE #73
Don't be afraid to stand up for yourself or speak your mind. It will not only earn his respect, in some cases it will even turn him on.

ATTRACTION PRINCIPLE #74
Men often automatically assume that a bitchier woman will be more assertive in bed, and that a nice girl will be more timid.

ATTRACTION PRINCIPLE #75
When a man falls in love, suddenly he'll go out of his way and think nothing of it. He'll do things for *this* woman he wouldn't have done for anyone else.

ATTRACTION PRINCIPLE #76
He'll never respect you as being able to hold your own unless you can stand on your own two feet financially.

ATTRACTION PRINCIPLE #77
**You have to show that you won't accept mistreatment.
Then you will keep his respect.**

ATTRACTION PRINCIPLE #78
**Your pink slip is maintained when you can stand on
your own—with him or without him. He should never
feel that you are completely at his mercy.**

ATTRACTION PRINCIPLE #79
**When a man views a woman as a "little girl"
or a sister he has to take care of, the
passion diminishes. He doesn't want to
make love to his sister.**

ATTRACTION PRINCIPLE #80
**The ability to choose how you want to live,
and the ability to choose how you want to be
treated are the two things that give you more
power than any material object ever will.**

ATTRACTION PRINCIPLE #81
**In a relationship of any kind, if one person
feels the other person isn't bringing anything
to the table, he or she will begin
to disrespect that person.**

ATTRACTION PRINCIPLE #82
Financial neediness is no different than emotional neediness; in both instances, he can still get the feeling that he has a 100 percent hold on you.

ATTRACTION PRINCIPLE #83
Regardless of how pretty a woman is, looks alone will not sustain his respect. Appearance may pull him in, but it is your independence that will keep him turned on.

ATTRACTION PRINCIPLE #84
When a man is very consumed with not being taken advantage of, this is a sign that he's "on the take."

ATTRACTION PRINCIPLE #85
People will show you they have self-respect simply by virtue of the fact that they *want* to carry their own weight.

ATTRACTION PRINCIPLE #86
The more independent you are of him, the more interested he will be.

ATTRACTION PRINCIPLE #87
If you make it too obvious that you're excited to get something, some people will be tempted to dangle a carrot in front of your face.

ATTRACTION PRINCIPLE #88
When you alter the routine, *your not being there* is what will make him come around. Men don't respond to words. What they respond to is *no contact*.

ATTRACTION PRINCIPLE #89
Don't give a reward for bad behavior.

ATTRACTION PRINCIPLE #90
He simply won't respect a woman who automatically goes into overdrive to please him.

ATTRACTION PRINCIPLE #91
If he doesn't give you a time, you don't have a date.

ATTRACTION PRINCIPLE #92
**Often the best way to adjust or fix the problem
is by not letting *him* know it's being fixed.
When you alter your availability or
change a predictable routine, it will
mentally pull him back in.**

ATTRACTION PRINCIPLE #93
Once you start laughing, you start healing.

ATTRACTION PRINCIPLE #94
**You can get away with saying much more with humor
than you can with a straight face.**

ATTRACTION PRINCIPLE #95
**A man feels he's won, or conquered a woman,
when she eats out of the palm of his hand.
At which point, he begins to get bored.**

ATTRACTION PRINCIPLE #96
**The *tension* that arises with a slightly
bitchy woman gives a subtle feeling
of danger to a man. He feels slightly
unsure because she is never in
the palm of his hand.**

ATTRACTION PRINCIPLE #97
A "yes" woman who gives *too* much sends the impression that she believes in the man more than she believes in herself. Men view this as *weakness* not *kindness*.

ATTRACTION PRINCIPLE #98
Be an independent thinker at all times, and ignore anyone who attempts to define you in a limiting way.

ATTRACTION PRINCIPLE #99
Truly powerful people don't explain why they want respect. They simply don't engage someone who doesn't give it to them.

ATTRACTION PRINCIPLE #100
The most attractive quality of all is dignity.

INDEX

A

abrasiveness, 241–42

accessibility, 5, 31–35,
    206–9

affection
    giving, 115
    showing in public, 66, 67

aging, xv, 241

appearance, xv

assertiveness, 47–51

attitude
    about self, 12–14
    independent, 237–42

attractiveness, 13–14

availability, 5, 31–35, 206–
    7, 208–9

B

bathrooms, sharing with
    men, 85

behavior
    danger-seeking, by men,
        234–35
    mothering, 37–41,
        126–31
    overly accommodating,
        233–34
    pulling back, 10–11

bitch

characteristics of, 20–23

communication style of,
    93, 94–96, 231–32

described, xii-xiv, 19–20,
    230–31

independent attitude of,
    237–42

je ne sais quoi of, 18–20

reasons men prefer,
    166–69

strong will of, 242–43

blame, shifting, 133–34

booty call, 33–34

boyfriends, talking about
    past, 72, 95–96

C

chase, thrill of, 26–37

chick flicks, 150–51

chores, getting help with,
    141–44

clothing, provocative,
    15–17

communication
    bitch style of, 93, 94–96,
        231–32
    male view of female,
        150–51
    talking too much, 93–94,
        152–56

M

male ego, 76–89
  making friends with,
    80–82
  making him feel manly
    and, 77–78
  maneuvering around the,
    83–87
  power and the, 86–89
  praise and, 79, 80–82
  public confrontations
    and, 86–87
Mama/Ho complex, 37–41
martyr, 146
men
  being taken for granted
    by, 128–30, 139–40,
    201–5
  danger-seeking behavior
    of, 234–35
  desire for challenge by,
    12
  desire for sex by, 59–61
  fear of losing freedom of,
    42–47
  figuring out hidden
    agenda of, 97–98
  helping to form good
    habits in, 90–91
  nature of, 26–27

pulling back behavior by,
  10–11
reasons for playing cool
  by, 156–60
thrill of chase for, 26–37
mental challenge
  altering routine and,
    199–209
  male desire for, xiv,
    4–5, 6
  renewing, 196–212
  sense of humor and,
    209–12
money issues
  appreciation for male
    spending, 185–87,
    190–91
  financial independence,
    174–85
  loans, 191–93
  paying on dates, 82–83,
    185–88
  splitting costs, 187–90
mothering behavior, 37–41,
  126–31
mystery, retaining, 21,
  95–96